THE
WHOLEHEARTED
MISSIONARY

100 Character Traits of the
WHOLEHEARTED
MISSIONARY

George Durrant

CFI
Springville, Utah

ISBN: 1-55517-897-9
e. 1

Published by CFI,
an imprint of Cedar Fort, Inc.
925 N. Main, Springville, Utah, 84663
www.cedarfort.com
Distributed by:

Cover design by Nicole Williams
Cover design © 2006 by Lyle Mortimer
Printed in the United States of America

10 9 8 7 6 5 4 3 2 1

Printed on acid-free paper

Contents

Introduction

Dear Missionaries:

I love to write to missionaries. I'm glad for this chance to write to you.

I have had many experiences with missionaries such as yourself. I served a mission to England when I was a young man. Later, I was a mission president in Kentucky and Tennessee. I also had the privilege of being president of the Missionary Training Center in Provo, Utah. Then, a few years ago, Marilyn and I were called to serve a church education mission in eastern Canada. I have also taught classes at Brigham Young University to help prepare prospective missionaries for their upcoming service.

As a result of these treasured experiences, I have learned many specific principles about how a mission can truly be a magnificent experience. I have written these short letters to you with these principles in mind. May God be with you as you read these messages from my heart to yours.

Sincerely, and with much love and respect,

George Durrant

1. *Your Mission*

Don't miss your mission

While I was President at the Provo Missionary Training Center, a homesick missionary, who had just arrived, wanted to go home. He asked me, "If I don't go on a mission can I still be married in the temple?"

"Yes."

"Can I still serve as a leader in the Church?"

"Yes."

"Then what would I miss by not going on a mission?"

I sadly replied, "You'd miss your mission."

You, as a missionary, know that to have missed your mission, with its joys and sorrows, its hardships and successes, and its opportunity to give so much to others and the Lord would be a loss beyond measure.

A time for a new beginning

A missionary who in his high school career had not been a great athlete, nor a student leader, nor popular with the "in crowd," arrived on a mission. He could tell early on that the local people, when they met him, were thinking, "I'll bet he was a great athlete. I'll bet he was student body president. I'll bet he was popular." The missionary did not tell them that their thoughts were not correct. Instead, he just acted the part they expected of him. He acted with the confidence of a student body president. He acted with the charm of a member of the "in crowd." He acted with the boldness of a star athlete.

A mission is a wonderful opportunity to start over in positive ways. The peer pressure of yesteryear can be abandoned. A new start in a new place where you are not known is an opportunity to escape what you feel others have made you and to become what you know in your heart that you can be. A transfer in a mission is also such an opportunity. Any bad habits and negative associations can be left behind and new habits and associations can be adopted.

2. *Be a Friendly Missionary*

Call people by name

Learn the names of the people in the ward where you go to church. If you serve in many wards, learn the names of the bishopric of the ward where you are going to attend church that Sunday. When you go there, call them by name. If you can't remember their names say, "Let's see, I know your name, but it has slipped me just now. What letter does it start with?"

"S."

"Hmm! Let's see. What is the next letter?"

"M."

"The next?"

"I."

"Oh, sure! How are you doing, Bishop Smith?"

The bishop would thus be impressed because you knew his name.

It is good to impress bishops. If you attend the same ward for a period of weeks, study the ward directory and learn as many names as you can. Calling people by name impresses them.

It is good to impress the people. If you impress them during your whole mission, your work will take on a new luster—a new success.

Never say that you are not good at learning names. If you say that, it will be true. Instead say, "I'm good at learning names, but I have to work at it real hard." Then go to work and learn the names. Study directories. Listen when people tell you their name. Ask those with unfamiliar names to spell their name for you. Make connections by saying, "Oh, I knew a person with that name. Are you related to the Smedleys in Cedar City?" Write down the names of people and go over the names later. Just trying to learn names will cause you to do the things that will help you do so.

Greet people

Greet the people at church. Get there early and ask the greeters if you can stand with them in the foyer to help them greet those coming in.

If you are shy, this will be a little difficult at first. But as you continue, it will become easier. With each greeting you extend, your return greeting will get warmer and warmer. Always start by reaching out, shaking hands, and saying something such as, "Good morning, I'm Elder ————. Who are you?"

When they reply, repeat their name. Tell them something about their name. Say something such as, "I've never heard that name before. Where does it come from? How do you spell it? I'm sure glad to meet you."

Pay special attention to the children. If needed, kneel down and be on the same level with the little ones. Ask them their names, and ask them to shake hands. Tell them to grip your hand hard. Then say, "Wow, you have strong hands. You are a good handshaker." If you win the love of the children, you'll win the love of the adults. Always remember that it is a thrill for people to meet a missionary, especially a friendly one. Give the people that thrill, and you'll experience the return thrill of greeting them. Tell them where you are from and how glad you are to be serving in their area. There is much good that a missionary can do by greeting the people. Do this just outside the chapel door in the foyer so you won't disturb the sanctity of the chapel.

In between meetings, while you are in the hall on your way to the next meeting, shake hands with every one who passes by. Tell them your name. Say something such as, "I'm Elder Smedley from Nebraska." Ask them why they look so happy. Be friendly, and your heart will fill up with love. You will radiate and, as you know, missionaries are supposed to radiate. It's your job to radiate.

Sit by people

You are always with your companion. It is sometimes a bit refreshing to get away from him. You can do that at church by not sitting by him. Find a family and ask them if you can sit by them. Maybe you can sit by a child. Open the hymnbook and share it with the child. It is great for you to sit by a child and share in feeling the Spirit of the Lord with him or her. If you and your companion don't sit together, you can do twice as much good. You are still with him because he is five rows ahead sitting by another child or by a lonely person who has just joined the Church.

Take an interest in the senior members

If you can't learn everyone's name in the ward, make it a priority of yours to learn the names of the older folks—especially the widows. Talking to the senior members is the best way to win the hearts of all the ward members. It is also the best way to win the heart of the Savior. On the other hand, try to ignore the young sisters. Say hello to them and be courteous, but save your best smile and greatest attention for the senior members.

3. *Be a Singing Missionary*

Sing out!

At church, when the hymns are sung, sing out. It doesn't matter whether or not you are a good singer. Sing out! If the Lord does not bless your voice, he will bless the ears of those around you. Hold your book out to the person next to you and encourage them to sing. Singing in church is a great thrill if done wholeheartedly. It is part of the blessings of attending church. People who love to sing the songs of Zion never fall away from the Church. Remember that, and tell the Saints that.

Sing for joy

Skipping and whistling are both signs of a happy person. You can tell that when a person engages in these acts the person is happy.

It wouldn't be appropriate for a missionary to skip. Others would consider that a bit odd. However, whistling is often appropriate. One of our happiest songs is, "Hark All Ye Nations." I defy you to sing this song without feeling happier during and after singing it than you were before you began. Try whistling that song while riding your bike. It will make the bike get farther per pedal than you were getting before you whistled out the first note. I can imagine you going down the side street of your assigned city with your hands off the handlebars just whistling the melody to "Hark All Ye Nations." On second thought, make sure that with your hands on the handlebars in a traffic area. You are too precious to take any chances.

Lift your voice and heart by singing

Happiness is like bread—it is best when it is homemade. You can't go to a store and buy happiness. You have to mix the happiness dough in your own hands and bake it in your own heart. You can do that by singing. You can even be a little like Tevye in *Fiddler on the Roof*, and just talk to yourself sometimes. Here is something you can read often, and it will lift your soul every time.

He Is the Way to My Best Day
I have every reason to be faithful.
I'm heavenly ordained to stay true.
Jesus Christ is my exemplar in everything I do.
He is the truth; He is the life; He is the way to my best day.
I have every reason to be hopeful.
I'm divinely endowed to ascend.
Jesus Christ is my enabler in every task I tend.
He is the truth; He is the life; He is the way to my best day.
I have every reason to be charitable
I'm celestially prompted to give love.
Jesus Christ is my provider of feelings from above.
He is the truth; He is the life; He is the way to my best day.
I have every reason to be happy.

I'm spiritually gifted to be glad.
Jesus Christ is my Redeemer from everything that's sad.
He is the truth; He is the life; He is the way to my best day.
He is the way to my best day.

—George Durrant

4. *Be a Dignified but Fun Missionary*

Have some magic tricks

When you go to a home, have a few simple magic tricks to show the children. Maybe you can pull your finger off, or at least make it look like you do. Maybe you can make a penny disappear into your coat sleeve. Your talented companion can help you with this. Or, ask for help at zone conference. There will probably be a missionary there who is a self-styled magician. Children love such tricks, especially when you don't do them well and they can see through your trickery. Also try to get good at singing Itsy Bitsy Spider, complete with actions. Ask the parents if you can teach the children a song. Teach them to sing, "I Am a Child of God." As you win your way into the hearts of the children, you will also win your way into the hearts of the parents.

Be at home with families

Be at home in the homes of the Saints and those you are teaching, but preserve your dignity. Be polite, warm, and complimentary. Pay attention to the family pictures and the décor of their house. Let them know how good it feels in their home. Tell them that you can sense that this is a gospel-centered home. Tell them that you can feel the Spirit there. Of course, you can only speak the truth. Pray to have some good feelings come into your heart about each family as you are with them in their home. Express these tender, heartfelt feelings with sincerity and your warm expressions will enter into their hearts.

Honor the head of the family

When in a home, direct much of what you do to the father. Honor him as the leader of the home. If there is no father, focus on the mother. If you desire to have prayer with the family, say to the father, "We would like to have prayer with your family. Would that be all right with you, sir?" When he agrees, you could say, "Because it is your home and you are the leader here, would you call on someone to lead in the prayer?" Advise him that he could say the prayer or he could call on one of the children to do so.

Honor the mother

Tell the mothers you meet about your mother. Mothers love to hear young people praise their mothers. They especially like to hear about mothers who have raised a son or daughter as wonderful as you are. Tell them some of the things that your mother did to help you in times of trial. Tell of her influence in your choosing to do the right things. Carry a picture of her, and show it to the mothers you meet. Tell them that you can tell that she is the kind of mother that your mother is. If you can make your way into the heart of the mother, you will have great influence in that family.

Pray for the family

Missionaries can do much teaching in the words of the prayers they express when they are in the homes. Be specific in your prayers—something such as, "Bless this good father that things will go well for him at his work. Bless him to be kind and considerate to his wonderful wife. Bless this good mother and help her to love her husband and care for her children. Bless little Johnny that he will grow up to be a great man like his father. Bless Sarah that she will always be good and virtuous. Bless this family with all the food and clothing they need. Bless them to always know the truth and to follow Thee."

Pray with the family

In one of the early meetings with a family you are teaching say, "Mr. Johnson, we would like to have a prayer before we go on. We would like you to say that prayer." He may hesitate. Slide from your chair onto your knees. Invite him and the family to kneel with you. Then tell him, "Just call on the name of Heavenly Father and then thank him for all you have." Tell him to name some of those things: his family, health, the good things of life. Then advise him to ask Heavenly Father for the blessings the family needs: protection from harm; health and happiness. Then invite him to go ahead. He will.

When you are back in your chairs, tell the children, "That was a beautiful prayer your father just said. If you ever need to know how to pray, ask your father, he knows how. He is a man of faith He is a great man who will lead you to do good."

Pray for the family to understand

When it is your companion's turn to teach his portion of the discussion, use your heart to silently pray for him and for those who are being taught. You can say such a prayer and listen to your companion at the same time. That which is orchestrated in the unseen world will be the power that will bring them closer to the Savior. Your prayers, even more than your words, will induce the spiritual music that will touch their soul and help them to remember again the things that they once knew and which are again entering the purest place in their hearts.

5. Be a Missionary Who Loves the Land

Be a "number one" Christian

In an indirect way, World War II, combined with other world events, opened the door for increased interest in Christianity in South Korea. During the period following the Korean War, I was there as a member of the United States Army.

Shortly after arriving in this land, I observed that some people were excited about Christ and his teachings. At the same time, the Koreans were confused because the good they had read and heard about Christianity was quite different from the questionable conduct observed in the soldiers who supposedly were Christians.

Korean civilians came into our camp each day to perform the menial tasks that were undesirable to us, such as KP. They, in turn, were paid, and the arrangements made both groups happy. As they went about our camp from building to building, they, like us, used the dirt paths that wound between the weeds and rocks. When American soldiers and Koreans met on the paths, the Koreans jumped aside into the weeds while the soldiers proudly passed by.

As I observed this situation, it occurred to me that this was not the way things should be. This was their land, and we, if anyone, should move off the paths. Therefore, I made it a practice to move aside and let the Koreans pass by on the path. This amazed them, and as they passed by me, I would smile, sort of bow, and give them a common Korean greeting: "Ahnyong hash imikka." As they went on they would look back with grateful expressions. They seemed amazed but also pleased at my actions. As time went by, I learned many of their names, and as they passed, I greeted them by name.

The American soldiers had created a system to communicate with the Koreans. Part of this system was to call that which was very good "number one" and that which was very bad "number ten." For example, if we were talking to a Korean about our good jeep, we would say, "This is a number one jeep." Or if it were a wreck, we would say, "This is a number ten jeep."

It was a rule at our camp that if a soldier held the rank of a corporal or higher, he would enter the mess hall and go to a table where a Korean worker would bring him his meal. All who had a lesser rank went through the line for their own food.

One day I entered the hall, noticed the line was long, and sat down at a table with five of my friends who were eating while I waited for the line to get shorter. As I talked to the others at the table, I felt someone at my elbow. I looked up, and standing at my side with a tray of food was one of the Korean workers. I realized that he was about to put the tray before me. To stop him from doing so, I said, "You can't serve me. I'm just a private!" All my friends at the table fixed their eyes on him.

He looked down at me with moistened eyes and quietly said, "I serve you. You a number one Christian!"

What that wonderful Korean man called me was not true of me then or now, but oh, how I long for it to be true one day. Sometimes I think I hover around four or five, but my dream is that someday

I can stand before my fellow men and before God as a number one Christian.

I know why the Korean worker judged me as he did. It was because of the little things I'd done. It's the little things that make a "number one" Christian. It is the little things that, when added together, make up the big thing called "life."

Honor the land where you serve

If you are in a land that is not your native land, learn to bite your tongue if the people criticize your land. Don't feel it a necessity to correct them about their views of the politics of your land or of the international relationship wherein they feel your country is wrong. Just move on to the Kingdom of God. If they criticize that kingdom then patiently try to help them come to an understanding. Keep your mind on defending the faith and let other things just pass by.

Love the people

Praise the land you are in. Praise the beauty of the mountains, the rivers, the spirit and greatness of the people. Express your gratitude for the kindnesses the people show to you. Do as did Ammon and say that you could stay in their land forever. If you try, you can truly love the land you are in and the people. When you develop this love, you will be able to have great influence with them. You will indeed have feelings at times that you would be content to remain there forever. Of course, there is no place like home, but for now, make the land in which you serve your land.

Declare your independence from the weather

A mission served in perfect climate would hardly be a mission at all. The weather is as important a factor on a mission as are the companions with which you serve. Without days of heat, humidity, wind, and cold, your mission would not have the value that a mission needs to have. The greatest of all decisions a missionary can make is to declare his independence from the weather. A missionary serving in Finland said that on the first day there, he was riding his bike into a cold wind and smiled at a person on the side of the road. His face froze, and that smile became the expression that he wore for the next two years. So let the weather, whatever it is, impress a smile on your face and, more importantly, in your heart.

6. *Be a Missionary Who Helps Others*

Build people up

Build people up. The world will tear them down. You build them up. Some people appear to be self-assured. Be assured that they have their insecurities. They need your support. They need your sincere compliments. Tell your mission president of your love and respect for him. At zone conferences, seek out his wife and tell her of how glad you are that you came to the mission where her husband is president. You could praise her, and that would be good. But the thing she loves to hear more than praise for herself is praise for her husband. Then she will tell him what you said, and it will buoy him up. Ask her for advice on how she has done so much in helping her husband become such a powerful priesthood leader. Tell her of your desire to have a marriage like they have. Asking her for advice is the greatest compliment you can give her.

In your personal interview with your president, tell him to take care of himself because you don't know what you would do if it were not for him being there. At the end of the zone conference he will be tired. Get him alone for just a few seconds and tell him how good it has been to be with him all day. Tell him of your deep admiration for him. Build him up so much that he will get a speeding ticket on the way out of the parking lot.

If you feel you can't do all of this, at least do a little of it. Every little bit helps.

Make others look good

Physical athletic competition is good, but keep it subdued while you serve your mission. If you are playing in an athletic contest, be more desirous to have a good time than to show how good you are and how determined you are to win. Once in a while, you will demonstrate a move, a shot, or a pass that will cause all to wonder. But don't feel compelled to show that you were once an "All American." If you hold back a bit, others will get the impression that you are far better than you are. Focus your ability on making another missionary look good, and that will help you feel good. Your job on your mission is to help others look good.

Be nice

One act of niceness can turn a dismal day into a joyous day. Let me tell you a story about when I was in high school.

It was in the early afternoon, just before we were scheduled to graduate, that I saw her standing with three of her friends. She smiled and asked me if she could write in my yearbook. I was astonished when she added, "Can I take it someplace where I can be alone?"

"You can do that," I said.

Finally, about half an hour later, she came back and handed me the book. I thanked her, and she replied, "I hope you don't mind my taking up a whole page."

I went home to change my clothes. Now was the time to read

what she had written. "Dear George." That was the first time she'd ever called me "Dear George." I read on. "I think that you are the nicest boy in the senior class." I'll have to admit I was a little disappointed that the first thing she'd mentioned about me was that she thought that I was nice. I had hoped that other things about me stood out more than my niceness. I had hoped she would write, "Dear George, You are the most athletic boy in the senior class," or "You are the most popular boy in the senior class," or "You are the most handsome boy in the senior class." Of course, such words would have been stretching the truth a bit. But in a yearbook inscription, that's not the world's greatest sin.

I guess having her list being nice as my leading quality was only disappointing because being nice had never been even on my top-ten list of qualities I wanted to be noticed for. It wasn't even as high as being studious.

The rest of her magnificent page went on to tell me what she thought a nice guy like me ought to do in life. She listed some things like college, a mission, and other things I'd not considered doing.

Now that high school has drifted into the past, being called nice sounds good. Come to think of it, I believe the greatest thing she could have said to me on that long ago day was, "Dear George, I think you are the nicest boy in the senior class."

I've lived up to all the goals she outlined for me on that page. The one that is the most difficult for me is being nice. If I could have but three goals come true, one of them would be to always be nice. That is a bit selfish because being nice to others always helps me to be happy, and when I'm happy I seem to be nicer. Then, before I know it, I'm right in the middle of my best day so far.

Compliment people on what they are

A lot of being nice is what you say. Saying things to people about their clothes, or their eyes, or their hair is nice. But a higher level of nice is to say things to people about what they are. You can get away with a lot of niceness by asking questions.

For example, you might say, "I've got a question for you."

"What is it?" they respond.

Then ask, "Why do I like you so much?" "Why are you so easy to like?" "What makes you radiate the way you do?" "Why does seeing you always make me so happy?" "Why do you look so happy?"

Being nice is best defined as not only not hurting people but also doing all you can to help them. Maybe the best definition of religion is just plain being nice.

Give people a note of praise

In school, you could get in trouble for passing notes around the room. It is different now that you are a missionary. While in church meetings, take notes on what a speaker or teacher says. Then give the notes back to him or her with some comments on how much what he or she said meant to you. You can be sincere if you sincerely look for the good qualities he or she displayed. Give him or her the note while at church so you will not have to take time out of your busy schedule to mail it. One written note somehow means more that any vocal compliment you can give. And giving written comments and compliments will give you a good feeling. A note to the bishop about the way he relates to the ward or to your investigators will mean much to him.

Remember the more you look for ways to make others happy, the happier that you will be.

7. *Be a Missionary Who Has Power*

Bring the Savior to the people

A woman called the Missionary Training Center and asked to speak to the president. She stated, "What do I have to do to get your missionaries to come to my house?"

The president asked, "Are you desirous of joining the Church?"

"Oh, no," she replied. "I'm quite content with my own church. But a few years ago, your missionaries used to come to visit our family. Their visits never convinced us to accept their teachings."

The president asked, "Do you feel like you now can accept their message?"

"No, it is not that. You see, the other night my husband and two of our sons got to talking, and we decided we never felt as happy as we did when your missionaries would come to see us. They always made us feel loved. They cheered us up. Their glow would remain in our house and in our hearts for days after they would visit. Now we feel a need to have them come again. Could you send them?"

We have two duties as missionaries. The first and foremost is to bring people to the Savior through baptism. The second is to follow the words of the great hymn, "Have I Done Any Good?" "Have I cheered up the sad and made someone feel glad?" If you do that each day, all along the way you have succeeded in deed.

Fulfill your major task of helping people come to the Savior. But don't leave the other task undone, the blessed task of bringing the Savior to the people.

Use Humor Wisely

A sense of humor is a virtue. It can also, unless used in wisdom, be a weakness. As president of the Missionary Training Center, I was advised by my General Authority supervisor to curb my sense of humor. I was told that it was not my role to be a comedian or to encourage the missionaries to be comedians. In the same session of advice, the leader told me to not give up my humor altogether. I was told, "You have a sense of humor that could be considered a ten on a ten-point scale. Cut it back to about a five. That will help you in your work and in your relationships with the missionaries."

That guidance served me well. I always kept my sense of humor around a five and it really worked. You could use that same guideline.

Each day, you will face many opportunities and many problems. As you do, you will need to discern, "Is this something about which I should laugh or about which I should cry? Is this a time to be sober or a time to lighten things up a bit?" Knowing when to laugh and when to cry is one of the greatest indications of maturity.

Some of the standards you could set for yourself are: First, I will never make light of sacred things, including other people. Second, I will never use any humor that will in any way take away the dignity of myself or another person. If I make good-natured fun of anybody, it will always be me. If you are funny too often, others will not take you seriously. On the other hand, if a sense of humor is really part of you, don't give it up; that would be dishonest with yourself. Just keep it around a five. The answer is to have balance in all things.

And along with the laughs, make sure you do some crying. The events and experiences of some days are heavy. On those days, cry a bit inside and, once in a while, outside. If you are sensitive, you'll be blessed with balance of the tender feelings of sorrow and humor, and with that balance you'll be both likeable and respected.

When with other missionaries

When you are with a group of missionaries, do not become too boisterous. Have fun. You deserve that. There is no better time for a missionary than when he gets to be with other missionaries. But keep your dignity under such circumstances. When you go down the sidewalk, make sure to leave room for others to pass by. In restaurants, be particularly courteous to those who serve you. Keep your voices down. When waiting in lines, watch for people who could be blessed by being allowed to go before you. Give up your seat on public transportation. If you feel other missionaries are a bit beyond the mark of dignity while in a group, quietly remind them to tone it down. They may resent it, but that is just the way it is. The best reminder is to make sure that you act that way yourself.

Lift others with your actions

There is powerful peer group pressure on a mission. Sometimes some lackluster missionaries try to use peer pressure to get more exemplary missionaries to comply with their less-than-satisfactory standards. When that happens, what do you do? First, don't act holier than thou in these situations. Use few words of criticism and then only when the time and spirit is right. Let your deeds do the talking. Don't participate in any activity that would take away from testifying. Perform to a high level of work. Have a sense of humor as you relate to the other missionaries. Don't act like they are all going to hell. Just make sure that you are not. When you do make verbal corrections, and you will at the right times, give your words power by what you do before and after you have spoken. One missionary can lift a companionship, a district, a zone, and even a whole mission. But he does not do so by condemning or criticizing. He does it by acting and loving.

Don't get carried away

This story happened many years ago. A gifted young college student who was intent on a certain field of study was grateful to be able to enroll in the class of a professor who was one of the world's leading authorities in that field. The student sat on the front row and was enthralled at each lecture the old professor gave. As do many of us, the professor had a few peculiarities in his manner of speech and his body language. Because of these traits, many of the students considered him to be quite odd.

One night the students were on a bus going down town for a night out. They were in a festive and light-minded mood. One of them began to speak in an accent like that of the professor. He mimicked other personality traits of the old fellow. The other students were all laughing heartily. Others joined in to add to the mockery. Finally, the gifted student got carried away and joined in the foolishness. His admiration for the teacher had caused him to listen and watch the professor so carefully that he knew his mentor's every voice inflection and mannerism. Using his expert knowledge, he did a remarkable job of mimicking his hero. The fact that other students were out of control with laughter egged him on to a more demonstrative portrayal.

Just then, he saw a man arise near the back and go to the rear exit. His heart sank, and he knew it was the man he nearly worshipped. He hurried back and got off the bus and stood by the old teacher. All he could say was, "Sir, I am so sorry." Tears filled the young man's eyes as the professor answered, "The others—yes. But you?"

Sometimes we get carried away when we are with others in an

informal setting. Never fall into the trap this young man did. Always act the way you want to act and not the way a group would encourage you to act.

8.

Be a Missionary
Who Loves Companions

Our pace, not my pace

One missionary told her president that when they went places her companion always walked so slowly she often had to look back and shout to her, "Hurry up." The perplexed sister asked the president what she could do to solve the problem. The president advised her, "Learn to walk as slowly as your companion walks. Then when you walk as slowly as her and love her at that pace, maybe you could gradually speed up so that your companion could, little by little, lengthen her stride. Just keep lovingly walking at your companion's side, and perhaps someday she will turn into a real speedster."

Love your companion's family

The second best way to really love your companion is to love his family. How do you do that when you don't even know them? Get to know them. As you walk to appointments, ask your companion to tell you about his family. Then as time goes by, when they write to him, ask him how his brother Zeke did in his school play. Ask him about his father's work. "Did he survive the layoff?" "How did the family vacation go?" If a letter comes which tells of his little brother making all state, go crazy about it. Say, "Wow! I'd love to see him play. Maybe I'll get to when he plays at college. He'll be a big star. Could you get him to write to me and sign the letter with his autograph? You are so blessed to have the family that you have."

Try to love your companion's family as if they were your own. You can't love any other family as much as your own, but you can love them a lot. The common desires you will share with him in the missionary work will be the main foundation of your mutual love. However, the common ground of his family will bring the two of you together like no other factor can.

It takes two

In the olden days, some missionaries not only rode bikes but also rode bikes built for two—"tandems," they called them. The missionary on the front was usually the senior companion. One time, two missionaries rode the tandem up a steep hill. When they got to the top, the missionary in front was exhausted and gasping for breath. He pulled over to rest and said, "That hill was so steep! I've never had to pedal so hard."

The other missionary replied, "Yeah, it was so steep that I had to keep the brakes on all the way up, or we would have coasted back to the bottom."

All missionaries are on a figurative tandem. If one pedals and the other just puts on the brakes by not being willing to help, then they don't get very far. When the two pedal together they can go up the steepest hill ever known to mankind.

Christ as a companion

To walk with Christ, you have to get up early in the morning and get going because He always starts His journey early. If you don't join Him early in the day, you will often feel empty and insecure and the pains of walking alone will fill your heart. You'll start thinking negative thoughts. You will remember past failures and feel certain failure will come again.

Do you ever feel that way? These are feelings you just don't want to have, but sometimes they come anyway. When you feel a little dark, you need to silently pray and say, "Oh, Lord, please let me walk with thee." If you say that and get up early enough to walk with Him, then everything changes. At least everything starts to change. Now the path can still be thorny and the wind can still blow against you, but inside you'll feel your spiritual and emotional power start to return.

One prayer that is always answered is the prayer for the strength to begin to make a spiritual comeback. Sometimes when you feel yourself drooping and your shoulders sagging, imagine you are walking with Christ. When you see Him walking at your side, you'll straighten up your shoulders and you'll walk as tall as you can. The journey will then be filled with light.

Not "I" but "We"

"I" is a good word. It helps us describe certain things from inside ourselves. Our personal study, personal worthiness, and inner sorrow or joy are all things that can best be described by saying "I feel . . ." or "I did . . ." or "I will . . ."

"We" is another equally good word. It's not as personal as "I," but it is sometimes more powerful.

Missionary teaching, tracting, or baptizing can only be accurately described by starting with the word "we." "We did . . ."; "We said . . ."; "We prayed that . . ."

Sometimes when describing our missionary work, we say, "I told the contact . . ." or "I decided that we'd . . ." or "I think I can get him to . . ."

If that is the way you describe missionary work, you have problems. You will be forever miserable, self-centered, and, in a sense, a failure. When you say "I told our contact . . ." and your companion hears it, he is wounded. Nothing hurts more than helping or trying and then being cut out of everything by hearing a companion say, "I had them read Moroni 10:4 . . ."

Instead say, "We told our contact . . ." or "We had them read Moroni 10:4 . . ." By saying we, you also include the Savior.

If you ever do want to give personal credit say something such as, "My companion, Elder Smedley, was really inspired when he challenged them to pray about their wayward son. That changed everything."

If you do want to use the word, "I," perhaps you could do so by saying, "I just happen to have the best companion in the entire mission."

You are responsible for each other

I recall this personal experience:

> When I was a missionary, my companion and I were crossing a small footbridge spanning a river that ran through the city where we labored. Because the bridge was bordered on each side by a high wooden fence and because it turned at an angle just before it ended, it was not possible to see the other side until one turned the corner. Signs were posted, "Do not ride bicycles on the bridge." My companion would put his foot on the pedal, push off with his other foot, and coast. I repeatedly asked him not to do that.
>
> One day, as usual, he did it again. He was about twenty yards ahead of me. He went around the corner and came face to face with an English bobby [policeman]. I arrived on the scene and said, "Officer, if I've told him once, I've told him a

hundred times not to do that."

My companion looked at me and seemed to be saying, "Thanks a lot, friend."

The officer, sensing the humor, smiled and said to him, "Now listen carefully, young man. I'm releasing you in the custody of your friend." He then turned to me and said, "From now on, you're responsible for him."

I've never forgotten that experience. And, by the way, neither has my companion. Many years later, I still, remind him that he is in my custody. He still reminds me that he really appreciated my thoughtful assistance.

But, you know, that police officer was right. I was responsible for him because he was my companion. And he was responsible for me because I was his. If you save one hundred souls but let your own companion slip further and further away, you're failing instead of succeeding.

If you let him spend his time, hour after hour, doing things unrelated to the proselyting effort, you are failing. If you let him spend undue time visiting members or others just for relaxation, you are failing. If you don't stay with him but let him be alone with girls or women, you are failing. If you let him get by without studying both the scriptures and the discussions on an almost daily basis, you are failing. If you let him stay in the apartment when you should be out proselyting, you are failing.

We all want to be liked, to be accepted, to be tolerant. But there must be a balance. If we want to become like our Father in heaven, we can't just wink at our companion's weaknesses and let him continue on his way to misery. We must stand up and say, "Elder, I can't do missionary work this way. Let's talk it over. I refuse to be a part of this. I feel our president needs to know what we are doing, and unless things change, I intend to tell him."

I'm not talking in terms of senior and junior companions. Juniors must help seniors and seniors, juniors. We need to be partners more and leader and follower less. We need to mutually plan and mutually aid one another toward a more excellent way. We all have weaknesses, so we can't justifiably nag one another. But we also know when someone is really out of line. When we know, we must act. Your companion's mission and perhaps his eternal destiny is in your hands.

As that police officer said to me, I say to you, "From now on, you're responsible for him."

The joy of companionship

As a mission president, I once told my missionaries, "On my wall is the big chart that holds each of your pictures. To look at the whole board is confusing. It's just a sea of faces. But when my eyes focus upon you—just you—I have a feeling of love sweep through me."

I continued, "Oh, how often I have wished I could be your companion! We'd really get them—you and I. We'd be the two best average missionaries here. We'd goof off, but only when the time was right. We'd bear testimony to each other. We'd study, but you'd have to help me because I'm not as smart as some. We'd go looking for people each morning. Sometimes we'd feel a little discouraged, but we'd go out anyway. We'd love the members, and they'd know it. We'd act in such a way that they'd say, 'Don't let the president ever move you two.'

"We'd teach some great discussions and a few that weren't so great. Sometimes we'd really teach by the Spirit. We'd be good friends with the bishop or branch president. He'd like us a lot. We'd write to each other's parents and encourage them. I'd write to your girlfriend. We'd eat pretty well, especially pancakes. We'd be sort of self-starters. We'd both want to become successful. We'd get a little discouraged if that didn't happen, but we'd keep working hard anyway.

"Then one day you'd get transferred. I'd help you pack. You'd tell people good-bye and they'd cry. I'd wonder if people loved me as much as they did you. We'd go the bus. We'd shake hands and I'd feel like crying.

"'I'll see you,' I'd say. 'Remember, we're going to room together at college. And remember at my wedding you'll be my best man.' Then you'd go.

"I'd go home and wait in the apartment. At 3:45 another bus would come into town. This time, another one of you would come into town and we'd start all over. Just you and me—companions."

I concluded, "I love you, my companions. Together we'll be what we ought to be."

Give the greater part

Elder Katmatsu tells the story of two missionaries stopping one morning at a fruit stand and each buying a big red juicy apple. One elder ate his apple as he rode his bike back to the apartment. The other saved his and put it in the fridge. The two then went back out to find and teach. In the late afternoon, they were nearby, so they returned to their apartment for a quick snack, but their food supply was meager. After eating a peanut butter sandwich, the one who had saved his apple took it from the fridge and began to polish it as the other one looked on longingly. Then the owner took a paring knife and cut the apple into two parts—one noticeably larger than the other.

The other missionary hardly dared hope his companion would offer him even the smaller piece. He was astonished as his companion extended to him not the small piece but the large one. The receiving missionary later tearfully expressed, "When my companion did that, just for a moment, I thought he was the Savior himself."

Change the contentious atmosphere

There was once a man who attended church leadership meetings where the leader encouraged open discussions before he made very sensitive decisions. Sometimes strong opinions were voiced, and certain individuals in the meeting even seemed to be at loggerheads with others.

During such heated discussions, a certain leader would be asked to voice his opinion. This sensitive man would say, "I really respect all that has been said. I just want to add a thought. In the spring of the year 1820, a young man walked into a grove of trees to ask God what he should do and what church he should join. As he prayed, he saw a bright light and in that light he saw two personages—God the Father and His Son, Jesus Christ." He would then briefly tell with warmth and love the remainder of that remarkable story. When he would finish there was always a transformation. The meaningful discussion still continued. However, a different spirit permeated the remainder of the discussion. Solutions were arrived at with the goodwill of all intact.

It is amazing what can be accomplished during trying times if we step back for a moment and consider our spiritual roots, our mission, who it is we represent, and what our message really is.

No other success can compensate

A great indicator of the success of your mission will be the success your companions have when they work with you. Sometimes missions are hard for missionaries. They just can't seem to get into the work with any great desire. It is difficult for you as their companion to help them because they do not want to give their whole heart to the work. You can see all that could be done, and you feel your companion is holding you back. Under such conditions, you will need to reevaluate what you are trying to accomplish. If you spend your time being frustrated about what you can't do, there is little hope of making some improvements in the quality of your companion's experience. If you can't do all you desire to do, then have as your greatest desire to see if you can help your companion do more and be better than he has ever been.

See success during this cloudy season of your mission as doing what you can do to aid in your companion's conversion. You can't do all things for him; however, with patience and prayer, you can do some things. This does not mean that you lower your standards, but it means you establish a standard of doing all you can for the one soul who needs your help more than any others—your companion. You can do it. Prayerfully go at it. Be proactive in seeking ways to help him feel the Spirit of the Lord. Teach him about love by loving him. Compliment him on the things you catch him doing that are good. If you try to help him, the Lord will help you. It won't be easy, but it will be among the most satisfying and important things that you will ever do on your mission and perhaps in your life.

9. *The Missionary and the Mission President*

No two are the same

Mission presidents are as different from one another as are missionaries. Some are "tough," others are "soft." Some are conservative, desiring each missionary to "toe the line," and others are lenient in the specific direction given to their elders and sisters. Some are more adept at teaching, and others have talents in organizing and administering programs. Some are constantly praising the missionaries. Others give few compliments. Some have been businessmen, some teachers, some doctors, some lawyers, and some farmers.

One of the most exciting and important things about your mission will be which of all of these kinds of men you will get as a mission president. The only thing that is certain about who you will get as president is that you'll get the president who is exactly the right one for you."

The president's feelings about his missionaries

Your mission president has something that you do not have. I see it this way:

> A few years ago, when my son Dwight (we call him Crow) was younger, I took him from Salt Lake to Provo. While I worked at BYU, he played with friends in the neighborhood where we had once lived. At day's end I picked him up, and we drove toward home. We stopped for a snack. We took our order from the cafe and walked about twenty-five yards to the bank of the Provo River. There, sitting on a log, we ate. I looked at the river and then at Crow, who was on the other end of the log.
>
> I spoke. "I've got a better hamburger than you."
>
> He answered, "Mine's just like yours."
>
> I added, "My milkshake is better than yours."
>
> He replied, "Mine's the same flavor as yours."
>
> After a pause, I looked at him and said, "I've got one thing that you haven't got."
>
> He was certain that I didn't have, and asked with a challenge, "What?"
>
> "I've got a son that I call Crow. And I'm sitting on a log with him and I love him with all my heart. And you don't have that."
>
> Crow didn't answer. He just looked at me for a few seconds, then he bit into his hamburger and threw a rock in the river. I had him, and he knew it.

I told this story to his missionaries and then added, "You missionaries are younger than I am. Many of you are smarter than I am. You have got so much more potential than I have ever had. But," he added with emotion, "I've also got something you haven't got. I've got nearly two hundred missionaries whom I look upon almost as sons and daughters. Missionaries who I love in a manner that I had never before dreamed possible. And you haven't got that." The triumphant president added to himself, "I have them, and they know it."

Impress the president

As mission president, I once said this to my missionaries:

Write to me each week. Tell me of your successes. When we are together, tell me what is in your heart. Help me to know you. Don't hold back or hide your real feelings from me. My desire to see you succeed is completely pure. Your success and mine are one. In order to help, I must know you. Don't hold yourself back, striving to not impress me. Go ahead, impress me. Impress me with the fact that you trust me and are willing to talk to me. Impress me with the fact that you love the Lord and have faith in him. Impress me with the fact that you want to repent. Impress me with the fact that you are glad that you are here. Impress me with the fact that you want to be recognized as being capable. Impress me with the fact that you like who you are. Impress me with the fact that you're doing good and want with an intense desire to do better. Impress me with your words. Impress me with your deeds. I love to be impressed. My joy comes when I can say, "You know, you really impress me." After all, to impress someone is to cause him to love you more than he did before. To not want to be impressive is to not want to be a child of God. And the greatest impression you can give is that which comes from being and doing good.

Use the president in your resolve to do good

When you are interviewed by your president, tell him of your problems. If you are not getting up on time, tell him. If you have problems with negative or impure thoughts, tell him. If you are staying in your apartment too much, tell him. If you feel you are getting to lax in your association with the young women in your area, tell him. Trust him. Make promises to him about what you will do to correct the problems. Say something such as, "President I've been sleeping in. I promise you that between now and the next time we meet, I will get up on time every morning." Ask him to write it down and to ask you about this the next time you have an interview. Just doing these things can help you change the quality of your mission. Your president's work is to help you have a quality mission. However, he can only do this if you trust him—if you will let him into your life.

Have a man-to-man relationship with your president

When you have had the part of the interview about your personal welfare and the work in your area with your companion, sit back and say, "President, we have been talking about me. How are you doing? You know, President, I really admire you. How did you get to where you are? What is the secret to having a life like you have? How did you find such a great lady to love and to marry? My dream is to be like you."

He will lean back in his chair and say, "Hmm! We only have a few minutes; however, here is what I think matters most in life and in the gospel." On and on he will go. It will be a conversation not between a big guy and a little guy. It will be a conversation between two men looking not up or down at the other but looking straight across as one man to another. You can have that kind of relationship with your president, and when you do you will have quite a mission.

Be a bit in awe of your president

A returned missionary said,

> The many ideals that are so much a part of a mission experience made words such as trust, respect, and confidence more important than things I had formerly dreamed of and which bore labels such as popular and all-state. Whereas before I had dreamed of personal glory and applause, on my mission my most intense desire was that my president would think well of me.

You, because you are a little different from me, may not fear authority figures. You might say, "Why be nervous around anyone, including the president? After all, he's a person just like me." The honors you have achieved and other fulfilling events in your past experience might have so filled your life that you stand in awe of no man. But as your mission unfolds, you will, if you are truly blessed, come to have a great respect for your president. And you too will feel a special tingle of excitement as you enter a private room to be interviewed by this man who has so much to do with all your mission hopes and dreams.

Respect your president's justice as well as his mercy

Sometimes in life justice is the kind thing to do. If missionaries are out of line, it can't be ignored. Discipline is necessary, and sometimes punishment must be administered. This story, which illustrates the role of justice, happened to me when I was a young man.

> At National Guard summer camp, I was the supply sergeant. I was to pick up rations on Saturday for Sunday. But our team was in a championship softball game, and so, contrary to the captain's orders, I had the supply clerk pick

them up. After the game, I checked with the clerk, and to my relief I found out that he had obtained the rations. So all was well.

Monday morning, I received word that the captain wanted to see me. He said: "Sergeant, I was very disappointed in you Saturday. You've always come through for me, and I've been one of your greatest supporters, but Saturday you disregarded my order."

"Sir," I replied, "you knew about the ball game, and you knew that with your help the clerk could get the rations. Why are you making such a big deal out of this?"

"It's always a big deal when orders are disobeyed." He looked at me, and I returned his stare.

After a few seconds, he said: "You leave me no choice. I'll start the proceedings for you to be reduced in rank." He stood up. He came around the desk and shook my hand. As he did so he said, "I like you. I like you more than you'll ever know." I could see his eyes moisten as he looked into mine. I sensed that the pain he felt was not because I had disobeyed the order but rather because he had had to punish me.

Somehow I sensed that the captain, with his kind, love-filled justice, had done the right thing.

How do you feel about this story? Whose side are you on? If you're on my side, I'm disappointed in you. I believe the world needs more people like the captain, more people who don't let mercy rob justice.

The easy thing for him to do would have been to say: "I've thought it over, and I'm probably being a little hard on you. I know how much the game meant. I know you won't disobey me again. So let's forget the entire matter." If he had done that, neither he nor I would have better understood the value of justice.

My tendency, and I feel you are a lot like me, is to not hold fast when someone's best interest would be served better not by mercy but by justice. It's not every day that we nonjudges need to administer justice, but when such a day comes, I hope I'll have the strength of the captain. I hope I'll look not at the day at hand but at the days that are to come. I hope that I will be willing to be fair but firm today so that I might help someone have a more fulfilling future.

Mercy is the best solution usually, but some days only justice will do. Painful as it may be to both parties, justice alone must prevail.

Be grateful when your president administers justice in the mission. Pray for him because that is the most difficult and discouraging part of his service as your president.

How do you feel about your president?

If a returned missionary could only be asked one question to determine the quality of his mission, it would be, "How did you feel about your mission president?"

If he answered something such as, "Other than my own family, I loved my president more than any person I have ever known. He caused me to desire with all my heart to be a good missionary and to dedicate my life to building the Kingdom of God." Such an answer would make it clear that that missionary had served a great mission.

Then the missionary could be asked, "Did your president ever do anything that you felt was unfair in any way?" After a pause the missionary might then say, "Well, not really. Except he did do something that at the time I wondered about."

"What was that?"

"It seemed that every time there was a troubled missionary, he always assigned that missionary to work with me. That was a little hard on me."

Then it would be clear that when the president did not know where else to turn, he would turn to this missionary.

You could be that kind of a missionary. You could be the one to whom the president turns when he does not know where else to turn.

Then the missionary could be asked, "Did you ever do anything to hurt the president in any way?"

Again the missionary could pause and then say, "Not really, except one time, I made him cry."

"How was that?"

"It was when he took me to the airport to fly home. We said good-bye, and he was fine. But as I walked away, I looked back, and he was crying."

So serve your mission in such a manner that your president will cry when you leave to return home.

Now is the time. How do you feel about your mission president?

10. *Be a Missionary Who Goes Where the People Are*

Open your door and get out there

Your apartment is a safe place. It is even a good place to hide on days when you are feeling a bit insecure in the work. It is a place to sit and count things or move papers around. It is a good place to study until your studying becomes less and less effective. It's a place to pretend that you are in your office organizing and telling yourself, "Doing this kind of stuff will help me to be a good missionary and give me the knowledge and the faith and the love that will enable me to be successful."

One of the things that made Christ so successful was that He didn't have an apartment or an office to sit in. He was almost always out among the people. If you have a hard time finding Him inside, open your door and go out among the people. That is where you will find Him.

In missionary work, we talk of having the faith to "open our mouth" and the words that should be spoken will come. An equally important principle is to "open the door of your apartment" and go out among the people. It's out there that the Lord can guide you to the door you should go to—the door to which you should deliver love and hope and truth. It is impossible to go to the right door if you have not opened and gone out of your own apartment door.

Be a little crazy

Some missionaries try to figure out reasons not to go tracting.

Once a missionary came to me for an interview. As we talked, the missionary started to cry as he said, "My companion's crazy, President. He's crazy."

Concerned, I asked, "What did he do?"

The elder replied, "The other day it was raining. I mean, it was really raining. He said to me, 'Let's go tracting.' He was the senior companion. I said, 'We can't go tracting in a rainstorm.' He replied, 'We've got to go tracting.' So we went tracting, and there we stood on people's doorsteps with the rain coming down out of our hair, dripping off our noses—there we stood. President, he's crazy."

Shaking my head in amazement, I replied, "Oh, boy! He is crazy."

I knew the next missionary in for an interview was the crazy elder. I could hardly wait to see him. The door opened and there he stood in the door (the crazy one—the one who tracted even when it was raining). I arose and embraced him.

This is not to say that tracting in the rain is wise, but sometimes some missionaries don't even want to go tracting if there's a cloud in the sky. You shouldn't be totally crazy, but being a little crazy can make a big difference.

Love and fun can get you in any door

Meeting people can be fun and meaningful if your heart is filled with love. Consider this approach:

"Good morning, ma'am. I'm Elder Smith and this is Elder Matthews. I can see you are busy." (Her little boy just pulled the tablecloth off the table and broke three of the breakfast cereal bowls, and her husband was cross before he left for work.)

"Yes, I am busy," she replies. "I have no time to talk." (She begins to close the door.)

"I was just wondering who planted these petunias," I ask.

She replies, "I did, but what do you want? I'm busy."

"My mother grows petunias back home. Hers look just like these. I really miss her. I haven't seen her in thirteen months. You see, I left home and came on a mission to tell people about the Lord's true church. But I sure miss my mother."

"I'm sure you do, but I haven't got time to talk about petunias." (She again starts to close the door.)

You, my companion—we'll call you Elder Matthews—see a little boy behind his mother and say, "Hi there. What's your name? He's sure a cute little guy. How many children do you have, ma'am?"

"Five."

"Five? That's the same as my family. I have a little brother just about his size. How old is he?"

"Three."

"What's his name?"

"Charlie."

"Hi, Charlie. Is that your doggie sleeping over there in the sun?"

"He's sure a fine boy, ma'am. You see, we are in the neighborhood calling on families. We have a great plan to teach families how to have a good time together. We know you are busy, but could we just come in for a moment?"

"Oh, I'm so busy, but I suppose so, just for a minute."

Once inside, I say, "Oh, who plays the piano?"

And you add, "Did your husband kill the deer and have the head mounted?"

We are almost in chorus as we say, "This certainly is a lovely home."

You can tract like that if you pray for love at every door. Perfect love casts out all fear.

Be humbly bold

There was once a missionary who was very bold and filled with love. When he entered a house he would say, "This house is beautiful." His manners were meticulous. He had the bearing of a king and the graciousness of a Secretary of State. Yet he had a common touch. He was fearless in asking people to live a Christlike life. His boldness in inviting them to come to church, to pray, to live the Word of Wisdom, to pay tithing, and to keep the commandments of God was shocking to his timid companion. This companion would think, "Don't push them so hard. They were just starting to feel the Spirit, and now you're going to offend them by challenging them to do all these things." But it would be the companion who would be shocked as they would say, "Yes, we'll do it." The people loved the bold elder. He seemed to know that "perfect love casteth out all fear." They knew that his boldness was founded on his love for them.

As the Lord's agent, change "timid" to "bold"

One fellow was so timid in high school that he could scarcely talk to girls. Once, in a moment of unusual boldness, he asked a girl that he really liked to go to a movie with him. To his surprise, she accepted. Together they walked to the theater. He hardly said a word to her. As they entered the lobby, he bought one bag of popcorn. They took their seats. He sat as far over on his seat as he could so that he would be as far from her as possible. He ate some popcorn, and it was delicious. He wondered if he should ask her if she wanted some. However, he wondered what he would do if she rejected his offer and said "no." So he hesitated. In his nervousness, he ate the whole bag himself. She was not impressed, and their dating was short lived.

This timid fellow was later called on a mission. And there he decided to change. He went forth in the name of the Lord, and the Lord helped him become as bold as he had once been timid. In the name of Jesus Christ, you can do the same. You can be bold even if at heart you are still a bit timid.

Speak for the Lord with boldness

I recall this story from my youth:

As a young high school student, I sat behind this dream girl in a history class. I wanted to talk to her and even ask her on a date, but I just did not have the courage to do so. One day my friend Don, who sat three rows over, sent me a note that said, "Ask the girl in the seat in front of you if she will go to the movie with me on Friday night."

With the note in hand, I boldly tapped the girl on the shoulder. She turned around, and I boldly gazed into her eyes. She smiled and asked, "What?"

I boldly asked, "How would you like to go to the movies Friday night?"

She smiled again and said, "I'd love to."

I boldly replied, "All right, Don over there wants to take you."

Why did I, who was usually so shy, on that occasion act so boldly?

Because I was speaking for someone else. I was at that moment an agent for another person.

Missionaries do not speak for themselves. They are an agent for Jesus Christ. They boldly speak in his name. They boldly testify in his name. They boldly challenge others to follow the commandments— to be baptized.

Talking to people wherever you go

A missionary wrote to me of this event:

I saw a young man at McDonald's. He was eating a hamburger, and I, a Big Mac. His hair was short and he wore a white shirt and tie. I came within a gnat's eyelash of saying: "Hi, there. I was wondering if you are a Mormon missionary."

He would have said, "No, I'm not."

Then I'd have said, "Well, you sure look like an elder in the Mormon Church."

"Do I?"

"You sure do. You look like a real winner, and that's the way they look."

"Well, thanks for the compliment."

"Anyway, I'm a Mormon missionary. What do you know about the Mormons?"

"Not much."

"Seeing as how you look like a missionary, my companion and I will come by your home and talk to you. What's your address?"

And then the Elders would have taught him, and then he'd have been baptized and his wife and her parents and her uncle. And this man's sons would have gone on missions and . . . But all of this won't happen because the missionary only thought of saying something. Then he thought, *I'd better eat this Big Mac and keep my thoughts to myself.*

When the man walked out of McDonald's, the missionary felt regret. Later the missionary could not get the man out of his mind. He wished he could be back there at McDonald's and have a second chance. But he couldn't go back. That night he humbly prayed that he'd never miss such an opportunity again.

Unleash your heart

As a timid high school senior, I was thrilled that a certain young lady had agreed to go with me on a senior class sled ride. I had a fine sled, and knew that would impress her. A two-ton truck hauled all the seniors up the canyon to a place they could board their sleds and head a mile or so down the canyon.

I told the girl to board the front of the sled, and I took his seat behind her. To my consternation, we had not traveled far when the right runner on the sled collapsed, and we crashed into a heap. There was nothing we could do but go back to the truck and sit in the back and wait. We huddled under a blanket to stay warm. Two other girls who had not dared to go down the hill were there. The three girls began to ask me about my plans after graduation. At first, I shyly gave short answers. But seeing the girls were sincere in wanting to know of my feelings, I did something he had never done. I unleashed my heart. I told how I felt about things. I told of my dreams for my life. I had never talked this way before. I had never felt so sincere.

The girl I liked had not been impressed with my sled, but I could tell that because of the feelings that I had put into words, she was now impressed with me.

I like the message the Lord gave to Samuel the Lamanite. "Go back and teach the people the thoughts that I will place in your heart." When a missionary finally decides to unleash his heart, that is when he begins to have power in his teaching. The Lord has promised us that He will place thoughts in our hearts. Then, if we have the courage to say these things, He will by the power of the Holy Ghost carry the truth of these thoughts into the hearts of the hearers.

Unleash your heart. A large percentage of the messages you will feel there will be messages of love, understanding, and faith. When you unleash your heart, you will speak the words of the Savior, and you will make it so that He can proclaim His message through you.

"Timid" soon becomes "bold" for those who unleash their hearts.

11. *Bear Your Testimony*

Bear your testimony at every opportunity

As Elder Boyd K. Packer said, "A testimony is to be *found* in the *bearing* of it" ("The Candle of the Lord," *Ensign,* January 1983, 54).

As a newly called missionary, I stood in the service station where I worked and excitedly told my boss, "I'm going on a mission."

My boss replied, "I'm glad you are going. It is better than college. It is better than the army. You'll learn so much. When you get home, you'll be more confident. You will be able to meet people better. You'll be able to speak and to lead."

Then his mood changed and he continued, "There is just one thing I'd like you to promise me."

"What's that?"

He replied with a bit of emotion, "When you get home, don't stand up and say that you know the Church is true. No one can know such things, and those who say they do are liars." I was a bit sad because I didn't really know the Church was true. I hoped it was, but I didn't know.

A month or so later, the district leader asked me, the newly arrived missionary, to give a talk in a forthcoming missionary meeting on the subject of Joseph Smith. I studied with more intensity than I'd ever done before. I prayed for the ability and courage to speak with clarity and power.

Finally the time arrived. Ten missionaries were assembled on the front two rows of the little chapel.

I stood to speak. My fear was soon replaced by other emotions. Something seemed to be happening deep inside my soul. I said, "And in response to Joseph Smith's prayer, God the Father and his Son, Jesus Christ appeared to him." When I said that, I felt a feeling that made me begin to cry. I tried to go on, but I could not. I looked down at the floor and sobbed. Finally, I was able to gain some control. I looked into the faces of my companions. They too were in tears. I was then able to speak again. I told of the persecution and the martyrdom of the Prophet.

I then sat down. But I was not the same person who had stood up, for now I knew. I knew that the message I was proclaiming was true. I knew that The Church of Jesus Christ of Latter-day Saints was indeed what its name says—the Lord's church. On that day I became a man.

Upon my return home, I spoke in a meeting where my old boss was present. I bore testimony of the restoration. Both of us knew that I was speaking the truth.

Truly a testimony comes in the bearing of it.

The missionary who was converted by his own testimony

A college wrestler whose girlfriend wanted to marry a returned missionary came on a mission without a testimony. His friends, especially his girlfriend, and his parents had encouraged him to come.

When he arrived, he told his mission president of his fears to serve because he was not sure of the message.

Two months later at a zone conference, he stood up to take his turn in testimony bearing. He said, "President, these have been the two hardest months of my life. Wrestling is a breeze compared to this. I've struggled with the scriptures and with the discussions. My companion is a great man, but I'm afraid we get on each other's nerves at times.

"The other night, we were teaching a man and his wife. This guy had been drinking, and he was sort of making fun of what I was saying. I showed him the Book of Mormon and told him about it. I told him about Joseph Smith. As I spoke, I could tell that he didn't believe what I was saying, but all of a sudden I realized that I believed what I was saying.

"President, Elders, and Sisters, I found out that I've got a testimony. And I want to tell all of you that this Church is true. I know that it is. I still miss my girlfriend, and at times I still wish I were home. But I'd rather be here doing this work than to be anywhere else doing anything else."

After a trial of faith

An elder told me, his mission president, "I want to go home."

"But," I replied, "You've only been here six months."

"I know," he answered, "but I can't go around telling people about something that I don't even believe myself."

I tried to get him to stay, but the missionary felt he was too honest, and he didn't want to be a hypocrite.

I asked him to read the Book of Mormon. He said he already had. I asked him to pray about it, and he said he had done so thousands of times. I asked him to stay another month, and he said he wouldn't.

I asked him what he'd do at home. He said he would probably get married.

"Won't she be disappointed that you came home early?"

He replied: "No, she understands. I told her and my parents that I'd try it for six months and then decide to stay or come home. So now I've done that. The Lord hasn't told me it's true, as he has all the others, and so I'm going home."

What is the problem in this case? Why hasn't this elder received a testimony? What could he do that he has not done? He came. He studied. He prayed. What does he lack?

Could it be commitment?

He was putting the Lord on trial and was not willing to endure his own trial.

He is on the verge of everything but is giving up just before he reaches the mark.

He needs to say: "Heavenly Father, I've really tried. But it's hard to continue without a testimony. I'm not going to go home. I'm not a quitter, but I need help. Please help me."

And then the trial would be complete and into his soul would come that quite wonderful feeling that indeed the Church is true. Jesus Christ is the Savior. Joseph Smith was a prophet. In striving to gain a testimony, we often come to know the truthfulness of Moroni's words wherein he said, "For ye receive no witness until after the trial of your faith" (Ether 12:6).

Bear your testimony to the members

Members of the Church don't ask the bishop if they can speak in church. But missionaries can. Ask the bishop if you and your companion can speak. When you speak, tell the Joseph Smith story. That story always touches hearts and brings the Spirit of the Lord into the souls of the speaker and the hearer. Tell the people about the role of the Savior in the great plan of happiness. Thrill them with your fervent testimony. Tell them of your love for them and for the Lord. Inspire them. Your job is to inspire people. You have been set apart to do that. You can do that. Do it. Sure, you are afraid at times. But remember that you don't represent yourself; you represent Him whom you are called to serve. Remember that He is never afraid, and you won't be either if you speak in His name.

Bear testimony when you are on your way to do something else

Much of the good the Savior did was when He was on His way to do something else. Do likewise.

A member of the bishopric quietly entered Primary to deliver a message to the president. He reverently approached her and gave her the message. She then asked him, "Do you have something you would like to say to the children."

"Oh, no," he said, "I do not wish to interrupt."

Then prompted by a better answer he said, "Yes, there is something I would like to tell the children." Standing as tall as he could, he said, "Joseph Smith went into a forest to pray. He knelt down and asked Heavenly Father which church he should join. In answer to his prayer he saw our Heavenly Father and His Son, Jesus Christ." He continued to speak from his heart as he told the children of his feelings about the restoration of the gospel.

Whenever you are in a home or at church and you are asked, "Is there something you would like to say?" always answer, "Yes, there is." Then tell them about Joseph's prayer. That story is your story to tell. It is your mission and everyone's mission to boldly tell that story. When we tell that story, it brings light to you and to all who hear you.

Assume that every person you meet has just asked you, "Is there something you wanted to tell me?" Then tell them about Joseph Smith or whatever else the Lord puts into your heart to say.

Offend some and convert others

A story is told that long ago, the missionaries in a certain town had decided that they should approach people with a message other than the Joseph Smith story and the Restoration. They felt that the story of the First Vision would alienate the people, and they would not allow the missionaries to continue to teach them. The missionaries were teaching many about good, nonoffensive things; however, in their hearts, they felt a degree of despair. They retired to a private place on the side of a mountain to pray. They appealed to God to know why they were not succeeding and why they felt discouraged. The leader, in his heart, heard a voice that said, "Bear testimony of the Restoration."

They hearkened to this message and boldly proclaimed that the gospel of Jesus Christ had been restored to the earth. Many who heard this message were indeed offended. But there were others who were touched by the Holy Spirit and knew that what they were hearing was true. The missionaries' hearts were lifted as they continued to do what the Lord had sent them forth to do.

12. *Be a Missionary Who Is Disciplined*

Dignity requires discipline

Some concepts are hard to express and are difficult for some to understand. So it is with the concepts that we call *dignity* and *respect*. A missionary showing dignity and respect calls his companion "Elder Clark." He knows that that is more appropriate than calling him "Clark" or "Robert" or "Robbie." He just senses that. No one needs to remind him. He calls his president "President" rather than "Pres." He does this because his inward dignity and respect causes him to sense that that is the way it should be. His manners are most gracious. Words such as *thank you, excuse me,* and *please* come quickly and sincerely. In someone's home, he sits with dignity. He's not a slouch, nor does he loosen his tie or try to act as though he's right at home because he knows he isn't.

He trifles not with sacred things. He smiles and he laughs,

but always with dignity and respect. He handles his scriptures, his garments, and his body with dignity and respect. He doesn't want the self-criticism that comes from a poor performance, and thus he prepares and works so that his dignity and self-respect are totally intact. Preserve your dignity and self-respect. No one else can do it for you.

Have the discipline to make pressure a servant rather than a master

I lived told this story about pressure:

> Our first-string center had just fouled out. The coach had no one to turn to but me. Not much time remained when I left the bench upon which I had spent almost my entire basketball career. With only seconds remaining the score was tied and I was fouled. All eyes were upon me as I placed my toe as close as I could to the line. Pressure bore heavily upon my shoulders. My beloved high school could win or lose, depending upon me. I released the ball and . . .

Well, you don't have to hear any more of that. But pressures are always upon those who go to the line and attempt to do great things. Every act of faith carries with it built-in pressure. Often faith requires an inward commitment that you are going to do something that is beyond your normal ability. And after a decision of faith you must ask yourself the soul-searching, pressure-packed question, "Can I do it?"

This kind of pressure is now associated with a decision you made that you will accomplish certain very difficult goals associated with helping people accept the gospel and become members of the Church. After the decision comes the pressure—pressure to be clean in mind and body, pressure to study and learn, pressure to pray with fervor and meaning, pressure to be more than you've ever been before, pressure to be worthy so that the Lord can do His work through you.

If you set no such goals, you feel no pressure. There are those who say: "Oh, well, I'm not going to worry. If we find someone, we will teach him; and if we don't, we won't." Or: "I do my best, and if they drop us, they drop us. I'm not going to sweat it." To such people, there is no pressure because there are no goals and thus no act of faith.

Pressure need not wear us down. It need not keep us awake at night. It need not cause us to have a nervous stomach. Pressure shouldn't break us down; it should build us up. Pressure is the soil in which great deeds grow. The way to handle pressure is found in the words of the song "Cast Your Burdens on the Lord" (*Hymns*, no. 110). There's a difference in casting your burdens on the Lord and not having any burdens. We should have goals and commitments to achieve certain things. Things beyond our ability. Things that put us under pressure—calm motivating pressure—and which prompt us to work and to pray with all our heart.

Missions make us better because missions are filled with pressure. And when we respond positively to that pressure, we grow.

I'm grateful for pressure. Oh, that foul shot. Well, what do you think?

Respect requires discipline

Happiness doesn't have much to do with what other people think of you, but it seems to have everything to do with what you think of yourself. If your opinion of yourself is less than favorable, you feel unhappy.

I recall this experience:

> Just a little more than a year had passed since high school graduation. A large group of my former classmates had gathered for a picnic. After eating a hot dog, I moved away from the group and stood alone under the giant cottonwood trees.
>
> A young lady who had gone to a car to get her sweater saw me standing alone. She came over.

For a few seconds, we stood together in silence. Then she spoke, "Quite a party isn't it?"

I replied, "Yeah, it sure is."

After another long pause, she spoke again, "You don't drink beer, do you?"

"No," I replied in an almost inaudible voice. I looked away from her and gazed out across the dark, calm waters of the lake. On a far shore, I could see the reflection of the burning flame of the distant steel mill. She spoke again with a tone of deep sincerity, "I sure do respect you."

With that she quickly departed and I stood alone. Over and over again in my mind I heard her words, "I sure do respect you."

Then to myself, I gently whispered, "I respect me too." I felt happy.

Discipline to do your best

A missionary had gotten off course. The president pondered and prayed. Should the missionary be sent home, or should he be allowed to remain? The two sat in a solemn interview. A decision was reached. The president asked, "Will you get up on time each morning if you are allowed to stay? Will you keep the mission rules with perfect exactness? Will you show your gratitude for this second chance by going far beyond what others do?"

The subdued missionary who was filled with hope said softly, "I'll do my best."

The president was a bit ruffled by this response and said, "Your best is not good enough. I want a promise that you will not just do your best, but that you will do all that you have just been asked to do."

There was silence. Before the missionary responded the president softened. "All right. You do your best. But, Elder, I just feel your best is far better than you have ever done so far. In the name of Jesus

Christ, you do your best. I love you, Elder. We all need to do our best. That is when the Savior steps in and does the rest and escorts us to perfection."

The elder stayed. He was true to his promise. From that time on, he did his best. He was quite a missionary.

Discipline to beat the clock

The alarm clock is like a good friend because every day it will tell you the truth. And in almost all cases, the truth will hurt. The clock moves so very fast during the night. Then with out warning, it goes off. As it does, it introduces a pain that hits you like a sledgehammer. The ringing truth tells you that morning has come. You can hardly believe that the sleeping pleasure of the night has ended and it is time to get up. You must now take the difficult task of getting up one step at a time. First, just slide out of bed until your knees hit the floor and you are kneeling. Then, in that humble position, say a short prayer with not much more than the word, "Help." Finally you are able to stand up. Slowly do so and then head for the bathroom. Every step you take will lessen the magnetic pull of your bed. After freshening up and gaining your strength, return to the side of your bed and assert your power over it by straightening its covers and laying the pillow in its place. Now try to force a smile. Just a little one; you don't want to break your face. Now try again for a full smile, and it will come more naturally. Sing a song or at least a verse. Something such as, "There Is Sunshine in My Soul Today." Tell yourself that this is your best day. Now the pain is gone, and because you got up on time, the day will indeed be your best day so far.

Discipline can make you look good even if you are not good-looking

Serving a mission makes a missionary more handsome. To make this true in your case, you need to look like a missionary. Dark suit, white shirt, dark ties, nice haircut, and shining shoes. But it's more important that you not only look like a missionary but also that you have a missionary look. To have that look, the Book of Mormon says that you should have the name of Christ written in your heart. Then you can have His image in your countenance.

I once had a wonderful day with my missionaries at zone conference. Following that long and spiritual experience, I went to a motel with my wife. When we walked in, the lady working there looked at me and asked, "Who are you?"

After I gave my name, she replied, "I don't care what your name is. Who are you?"

I answered, "I am a missionary for The Church of Jesus Christ of Latter-days Saints."

And she said, "Oh, I knew it was something special. I could tell by the way you look."

I winked at my wife and jokingly replied, "You mean because I am handsome?"

"Oh, no," the woman replied. "You're not handsome. As a matter of fact, you're not even good-looking. The thing I noticed about you when you walked in is you look good."

So you see, you can look good without being good-looking. That's the "look of a missionary." By having the image of Christ in your countenance, by having His name written in your heart, you look good. That is more important than your clothes. You can have "the look of a missionary" by being all the way into your mission with your whole heart, mind, and strength.

13. Be a Missionary Who Builds Faith in Jesus Christ

Faith is the foundation of confidence

I had a friend named Bob. He told me that one day on the farm, the tractor suddenly stopped running while he was working with it. He came to the house. His father, who was afflicted with arthritis, asked what was wrong. Bob replied, "The tractor stopped on me."

"Go fix it," the father said.

"I can't fix a tractor," Bob answered.

"Sure you can, son," the father said confidently. And then with a broad smile, he added, "All you've got to do is have the confidence to try."

The confidence to try, more than talent, seems to be the thing that separates those who get the job done from those who do not. You can do mighty things on your mission. All you have to do is to have the confidence—the faith—to try.

You can do it

Perhaps God's greatest revelation to you is that you can do it. This story happened to me:

> In high school, I'd never had the confidence to try to do things. A year or so later, I had an interview with my stake president. He had asked me several questions about my Church attendance, my habits, and my feelings. After I'd replied, he said, "We'd like you to be an elder. How would you like that?"
>
> I replied with great joy, "I'd like that a lot, President."
>
> After I'd said good night to him, I headed right to Don's Sweet Shop.
>
> Because of what had happened in my stake president's office, I was feeling good. The pretty waitress said, "Hi, George. What would you like?"
>
> "I'd like a cherry chocolate milkshake with more cherry in it than chocolate."
>
> As I waited for my shake, I felt friendly. I looked around to see who else was there. I nodded a greeting to each. As people went toward the door, I would catch their eye and say, "See you later."
>
> When it was ready, I sat sipping the delicious shake. My mind went soaring. I was having a silent conversation with myself. I thought, "I'll bet I could do stuff. I'll bet I could do college work and all that kind of stuff. I'll bet I could paint pictures and do all sorts of art stuff. And live good and pay tithing and do spiritual stuff and love everybody and help people and do stuff like that. I'll bet I could even go on a mission. It would be hard

for me because I sure feel timid about talking to people and that kind of stuff, but I'll bet I could. I'll bet I could really amount to something in life. I'll bet I could do a lot of stuff."

My thinking was suddenly interrupted by the noise milkshakes make when they are almost gone.

I paid the bill and said good-bye.

It seemed to me that that night and other times when I get to thinking that I can do stuff that I look better, feel kinder, act friendlier, and walk better with the Lord. Some days I feel down. On those days, something says to me, "You can't do stuff." I sort of lose my courage.

That's when I sing. Then I pray. Usually I hear a small voice say, "You can do it. All you've got to have is the courage to try. Get up and do it." And when I do that, it gives me confidence to do other stuff. Pretty soon I'm not only doing stuff that I'm expected to do for my work or my classes or my assignments, but I'm also doing more. Feeling I can do stuff and then doing it makes all the difference.

You can do stuff. Pray about it and you'll get a revelation that will say, "You can do it."

The main change is more faith

Long ago, I was called on a mission to England. I went from my little town to the mission home in Salt Lake City. There I had an immediate love for my first companion, who was also a small town boy. We two elders seemed to be on the same frequency and could talk to one another about our deepest thoughts and concerns. One day, we walked to a drug store to purchase some seasick pills for our upcoming voyage to England. As we walked back to the mission home, we had a very meaningful conversation filled with both humor and seriousness. When we were nearly back, he said to me, "I'm glad we've met here and have become friends." He then added, "Promise me that while you're on your mission, you won't change because I like the way you are now."

What do you think of that challenge? I did not reply. However, I never forgot my first companion's advice.

Two years later, while coming home, I wondered if I had changed. As best I could, I tried to determine whether I was still the same or if I was different than I had been. I determined that I was indeed the same old guy that I had been when I left my hometown. But as I thought about it, I realized that I was the same guy who my first companion had known. But, somehow, I was same old guy in a new way. People back home still recognized me as the guy they used to know because I still had the same fun-loving personality. But somehow, those who got to know me all over again recognized that my weaknesses had changed to strengths. I was more dependable. I knew what I wanted. I knew that I could succeed. I had more love, more consideration, and more integrity. I was more bold. I was the same in all the good old ways, but I was different in the ways that made me a greater instrument in the hands of the Lord.

The changes had come about much like the coming of spring. To see spring come, you must go out each day and measure closely each bud, each blossom, each blade of grass. Even under such scrutiny, spring will come, and you won't know exactly when. But somehow, when the transformation from one season to another has come, it makes you glad, and it fills you with hope for the future.

The missionary had changed. The main change was that he had greater faith in Jesus Christ and that, like sunshine to a plant, made all the difference.

Preparation brings confidence

A great basketball coach taught that confidence comes from preparation. He told his athletes that in order to feel they could win, they had to feel that they deserved to win. If they paid the price by making sacrifices and doing hard work, they would come to feel that they deserved to win. Such athletes had the confidence that they were prepared, and thus they lost their fear. Being a confident athlete is more powerful than being a talented athlete. You have seen players who were talented enough, but they were not confident enough. Feeling that you deserve victory is called confidence in athletics. It is called faith in a missionary. If you are prepared by study, prayer, and obedience, you will not fear. Your faith in Jesus Christ will enable you to know that you are not alone. You will know that you can call down the powers of heaven to assist you. You will know that you have done your part, and you will know that the Lord will do His.

Faith always leads to repentance

It's hard to single out one principle that is more important than others. But it seems that we all need desperately to be able to repent. There's probably no one quite as excited as the man who has repented and knows he's on the right track. There's a lot of forgiveness behind each missionary being on a mission. And now that you have received a remission of your sins through your repentance and baptism, how important it is that you remain clean and pure!

Joseph Smith recorded, "It was truly manifested unto this first elder that he had received a remission of his sins" (D&C 20:5). This indicates that when Joseph Smith prayed in the grove of trees, one of the things he received was forgiveness of his sins.

There has to be a grove of trees in all our lives, a time when we go before the Lord and lay it all out before him—what we've done and what we intend to do. Often, after having explained it to Him, He gives us the impression that we should talk to our priesthood leader. When this is done in the proper manner, when we have a broken heart and a contrite spirit, it's possible for us to receive a remission of our sins.

May the Lord bless us all that we might be able to teach repentance. We've all had some experience with it. The very purpose for our being here is to help each individual have sufficient faith in Christ to repent of his or her sins. There's no repentance without finally being baptized and receiving the gift of the Holy Ghost. And there's no place that this can be done except in the Lord's one true Church. We are the Lord's agents. This is His Church. We know that. We have experienced a mighty change, and we invite others to do the same.

Come to the center of the gospel

The blessings of the gospel are in the center of the Church—Jesus Christ. They are not on the edge. Move to the center and away from the edge. The mission rules, the counsel of your mission president, and the enticings of the Lord will all prompt you to move to the center of your mission. Move to the center, and you will feel a harmony with your leaders and the Lord. However, sometimes it is difficult to stay in the center. We are all prone to wander. When you feel you are moving away from the Spirit of the Lord—away from the center—come back. You will have to come back almost every day. Consider carefully each day whether you are moving away from or toward the center of the spirit of your mission. Build on the things that move you to the center, and avoid any attitudes or practices that take you toward the edge. The closer you feel to the Savior, the closer you will be to the center of the gospel.

14. *The Power of a Missionary*

The missionaries are nearby

I was filled with joy each day when I saw my five-year-old granddaughter, Lexie. My heart almost broke when she moved with her family to a distant state. Now I could only see her once a year. Every day I prayed that she would be safe and happy.

Then one day her mother called and said, "The missionaries here came to see us. You know how shy Lexie is around people. She's not like that with the missionaries. She shows off for them and even sings for them. She looks for them at church and sits by them. She loves them."

I was so happy that I sent a letter to Lexie and said, "Your mother told me that you love the missionaries. She said that the other day you were tired and lonely and you said, 'Momma, where are the missionaries?'"

I then answered Lexie's question. "Where are the missionaries? They are all over the world. They are the Lord's agents. They have pure hearts and clean hands. They are the hope of the world. You can count on them Lexie. They won't let you down. They love you and all children and all big people. They love Heavenly Father and Jesus.

"Where are the missionaries? They are wherever you pray them to be. I love you Lexie and I miss you. I wanted with all my heart to see you. So I prayed for your happiness. Heavenly Father said, 'Let's answer that grandfather's prayer. Let's send the missionaries to Lexie. Let's let Lexie know that the missionaries are to love and to be loved. Let's send the missionaries to Lexie so that she will be happy.'

"I love you Lexie. Someday I will hold you close again. Until then, my prayer is that when you say, 'Where are the missionaries?' That they will be near by. I pray that same blessing for all of Heavenly Father's wonderful children. I pray that the missionaries will always be nearby."

Time to start over

In the olden days, all missionaries took a large trunk filled with what they'd need on their mission. A perspective missionary could pack a lot of stuff in such a trunk. Today missionaries do not bring a physical trunk. However, they do bring a large emotional trunk filled with their past experiences and feelings.

Some come with a trunk packed full of confidence, boldness, and a dynamic personality.

Others come with a trunk filled with self-doubt and timidity.

It does not matter what you bring in your trunk of the past. Unpack your trunk by forgetting the past. The past is past. Begin to fill your trunk with hope. See a vision of the glorious future. Find a missionary who has the inner qualities that you desire. See yourself as becoming like him. Read of the Savior and do all that you can to be like Him. He is your Savior, not only when you die and appear at the judgment seat, but He is also your Savior now. He can save you from doubts. He can save you from feelings of inferiority. He can save you from discouragement. As you try to be like Him, He will enable you to fill your trunk with a vision of the future that will take away the baggage of your past. He will empower you to be what He and you want you to be.

The power is in you to be a leader

One day, a very sad day, a letter came from the mission office. The senior companion was to be transferred the next day. The junior was now to be the senior. For the last time, the two rode their tandem together—the senior on the front and the junior behind. At the train station, the shaking junior companion said, "I don't know what I'm going to do without you." Tears filled the eyes of each.

"You'll do great," the senior assured as he turned to board the train. Then he was gone.

Emptiness is the only word that comes close to describing how the junior felt. But he was not alone for long. The new elder arrived at the station. The two walked out and pulled the tandem bicycle from the brick wall against which it leaned. The new senior companion swung his leg over the unfamiliar front seat, and the junior climbed on behind. As they headed up the road, everything looked frighteningly different from the front. Now there was so much to watch out for. The senior felt desperate for direction.

The day the elder moved from the back seat to the front seat of the old tandem was the day he more fully learned that there's a third companion who sits on an unseen seat in the front. He learned that if we desire Him to do so, He will take His seat and off we'll go. If the hill we're going up is steep, we'll still make it to the top. If the weather is warm and humid, we'll still get through it. If it's cold and penetrating, we'll make it. If the people reject us we will be disappointed but not discouraged. If power to challenge and to testify is needed, he will grant it. This divine companion, Jesus Christ, will never be transferred, and if we desire Him to be, he will be with us always and we'll never be alone. This knowledge of the unseen companion is what makes a humble follower into a dynamic leader.

Time goes by

Your time is now flying by. You've been out for a while. Then it's eighteen months, and suddenly it's twenty months. "Slow down, time, please." Then twenty-two months.

You are now one of the "old men" of the mission. A new missionary says to you, "How long have you been out?"

When you tell him, he gasps for breath and says in complete awe, "Twenty-two months!" He almost reaches out to touch you. You're a patriarch. You're the person to whom others turn for advice, for counsel, for encouragement. You, who have met and discussed the gospel with ministers, doctors, and governors. Your president has placed trust in you, and you've been true to that trust. Your scriptures are well marked and worn. You humbly know that you are respected and loved.

Finally there are only twenty days left. Then ten. Then only hours.

You meet with the president for the last time, just the two of you alone. He says: "It seems as if it was just last week that I met you at the plane, and now you are going home. How do you feel, knowing that tomorrow you'll be home?"

Your reply: "President, I'm confused. When I first came, I thought it would never end. And now I just can't believe it's over."

A long pause follows as you look into the president's eyes and he into yours. A communication goes between you that can take place only between those whose love and respect is complete.

"You've been a valiant one, Elder."

"I've tried, President. I really have. I've not always been perfect, and I've wasted a little time now and then, but I've tried. When I first came out, I wanted desperately for the time to fly by so that I could go home. I missed my folks and everyone at home. Out here I've found myself. I've discovered who I am and what life is all about.

"President, I didn't know I could ever love any place the way I love this place. I didn't know that I could get so close to people. These people are my people. I don't want to leave them. I feel like they need me. I wish I could stay, but at the same time, I want to go home. I know there are things for me to do at home, but my heart is here."

Tears fill your eyes as you try to continue. "President, I'm confused. I want to go, and I want to stay. What do you think?"

"Elder, your work here is finished. In the past two years, you've captured some spiritual ground. Go home and never give up an inch of it."

The president continues: "I'll miss you here. We all will, but your life is now to go down different roads. Along the way, you'll meet the right one and marry her in the right place. You'll become a counselor in the elders quorum presidency. You'll become a father. You'll move to the Midwest or someplace. You'll become a counselor in the bishopric. Another child will come. You'll fall more and more in love with your sweetheart. You'll be a great father.

"In other words, you have a destiny out there. Now square your shoulders. Go home and get on with life."

Maybe at times disappointed but never discouraged

What is success for a missionary?

First let's discuss your success as a missionary. If you ever decide that the success of a mission doesn't necessarily correlate with the quantity and quality of new converts, then you will not be an effective missionary. A successful business renders a service or produces something worthwhile, but its overriding success is determined by its profits. An athletic team is successful when it wins. And a mission is a success if it is the means of bringing people into the Church, and that is the real and rather hard truth.

Some say: "We can't make converts here. Not with these people, not now." And thus, through their excuses they begin to feel comfortable. To have such comfort, they pay the price of lowering their goals. Their enthusiasm wanes, and they lose the great edge that is described as the missionary spirit.

Now, let's talk about your success as a man. If baptisms don't come, be disappointed, but don't be discouraged. There is a difference, you know. To be discouraged means you are losing courage, and that isn't the case with you. To be disappointed means your goals are not being met, and that's what you are experiencing.

A missionary's eyes moistened as he said to me, "I get the feeling that Mom and Dad wonder why we aren't baptizing anyone." Tears fell as he tried to continue. "They had such high hopes for me, and I'm letting them down. I try, President, I really try; but I just can't seem to do it." I sat silently as the elder softly cried. How I loved him! How I hoped that I'd have a son who'd care as much as he cared!

I found myself wishing I could look into the missionary's father's eyes and ask: "How did you raise such a son? How did you infuse in him such honor and integrity? How did you teach him to love so completely? How did he come to be so totally responsible?" I could learn many things from the father of such a noble son.

The Spirit of the Lord filled the hearts of the father and the elder.

The president knew he was in the presence of a man of God. Then the elder spoke again: "President, my companion and I will work even harder. I know there's a family waiting for us. We're going to find them and bring them into the Church. You just watch." Days came and went and the elder's full-time mission ended, and he hadn't found the family. But how he had searched and prayed and worked!

That elder was a successful missionary, for he was a real man. He wanted to find a family so much. It broke his heart when he didn't. But how he tried!

Keep being disappointed in your mission until baptisms come. And if some do come, then be disappointed if more don't come. And through all your mission disappointments, conduct yourself in such a way that you'll never be disappointed in yourself. And if that is your lot, then you, my dear friend, will have been and will forever be a successful man.

The Power of Being Happy

I feel this way about happiness:

In our society, the most frequently asked question (by a margin of 607 to 1) is, "How are you?" Or more expertly and warmly asked, "How ya doin'?"

The common answer to this most thought-provoking question is the all-encompassing word, "Fine."

But to respond solely with "fine" is the most noncreative, nondescriptive, unexciting, blah answer ever devised. Being just fine places you about six-and-a-half miles short of being happy.

Feeling as I do about the word *fine*, I have for years searched for a better answer. For a time, when asked "How ya doin'?" I experimented with the answer "Champion!" When that lost its appeal, I switched to "Superb." When that began to sound hollow, I changed to "Not half bad." (That is a British approach.) But never was my thirst for just the right answer quenched.

Then one day when I was feeling so full of joy that I could scarcely contain it, someone asked me, "How are you?" And without even thinking I blurted out, "My best day so far!" As I continued on my way, it suddenly occurred to me that I had just found the answer that I had been seeking for so long.

Let's try it and see what you think. You ask me, "How ya doin'?" I'll reply to you, "My best day so far!" What do you think? Isn't that the most perfect answer that you've ever heard? Try it today. Try it every day. It can change your mission and your life.

Compared to yourself

I once lived this story:

One day I climbed Mt. Olympus. It was an

unbelievable, long, hard and exhausting journey for me.

Later that day, I attended an early evening meeting at our chapel. Every muscle in my body ached. I could hardly walk. My face was sunburned. After that meeting, I went out and looked up at Mt. Olympus. It looked different now that I knew I had been to the top. I was so deeply proud of what I had done. I sensed then that a man was standing at my side. He asked, "What are you looking at?"

I said, "Mt. Olympus." Then, in an almost bragging way, I said, "I've been to the top of that today."

He said, "Oh, really! That's great." Then he added, "I've been up there eighteen times."

"Eighteen times," I said. "Boy, that's really something."

He said, "Which way did you go—the easy way up back?"

I said, "Well, we went up back."

He said, "That's the easy way." After a brief pause, he continued, "I go right up the face." I kept gazing up. Suddenly I realized that what I had done was no major accomplishment for anybody else, but it was only a major accomplishment for me.

I thoughtfully turned and limped away. I wasn't in competition with him or anyone else. I was only in competition with myself, and that day I had been a winner. In the days and weeks that followed, I would look up at the lofty peak of Mt. Olympus and think, "I've been up there. Not to that lesser peak off to the right, but to that higher one—the top one—the one I said I'd climb, and I did." Even now when I see majestic Mt. Olympus, I'm filled with the reward of that climb again and I say to myself, "I'm sure glad I didn't turn back."

Even though the day that I climbed Mt. Olympus was a great day, today is far better because today there is a new mountain to climb. Each day's mountain is different, but each day has within its hours a special mountain for each of us to climb. Today's mountain may be an upward slope through forests of fear, climbing under the hot sun of tedious tasks, or across sheer boulders of my own expectations. Or it may be down a painful slope strewn with the loose and slippery rocks of selfishness or the entangling roots of pride.

But though sometimes I must rest and gasp for emotional breath, I must move forward. And though the downward momentum of unfulfilled hope may slam me to the ground, I must get up and go on to my goal. Others have their challenges and I have mine. The only accurate measurement of success for me is how do I compare with myself and the goals that I long to achieve. Am I climbing my mountain and getting ever nearer to the top?

Hope

Hope is among the most tender of all feelings. It is the foundation of all happiness.

What if hope dies? Then what?

That question isn't worth considering, because hope never dies. It is always there. God sees to that. Maybe on the darkest of nights and in the saddest of experiences, hope will be a flicker so small that it can scarcely be seen. However, it will still be there. It's small. Every burning flame needs only to be fanned, and it will flare up to a glorious and radiant light.

Having great hope is only surpassed as an ingredient of happiness by the joy-filled process of giving hope to others.

When I was a young man, the Lord taught me about hope by letting me sit on the bench as a high school athlete. He taught me how it feels to be on the sidelines when I wanted to be in the middle of the action. Through that and other disappointments, my flame of hope dimmed. I wondered why I had to endure such discouragement. But these things gave me vital experience. I learned to treasure hope.

Now because I know how it feels to have a lack of hope, my greatest desire is to give hope to those who feel despair.

One of the important things in life is to find people who are sitting on life's dismal benches and say to them, "Come on, stand up and get in the game."

Perhaps they will say, "Why should I? Besides, what do you care?"

And you can reply, "I care because I love you. I need you and so do others. Now get up and get going. You can do it."

Maybe when someone says to you, "Have a nice day," what they are really saying is, "Have a day filled with hope and a day of giving hope to others." Go forward today by adding fuel to the flame of hope that burns too little in some person you meet along the way, as you teach, at church, or even your own companion. If you have a day wherein you fan the flame of hope in others, you will feel much hope and love in your own heart.

Teaching

A mission is the time to learn the greatest of all skills. It is the time to learn to be a teacher. It would be good for you to someday become a brain surgeon, or a builder of great bridges, or a microbiologist. Maybe you have the talent to be an artist or a musician. Perhaps you will be an executive of great renown. You could do much good by being a craftsman. But no accolade you could ever receive is as lofty as that of being referred to as a "master teacher."

To become a master teacher does not mean that you will need to come home and become a seminary teacher or a public school teacher. It could mean that for you. But what I mean is that whatever field you enter to make a living and a contribution to others, you will still have many opportunities to teach many things, especially the gospel. And the thing that will be of most worth to others is the manner in which you teach them the gospel.

While you are serving your mission, you should have an insatiable desire to increase your ability to teach. Every time you teach, ask yourself, "How could I have taught that better? What better examples could I have used? What did I do that made them respond so favorably?" Ask your companion how you can improve as a teacher. Study the scriptures so that you will have power. Speak from your heart in the spirit of truth. Express your love and the deep feelings of your heart. Teaching the gospel has a unique quality that no other teaching has—the Holy Ghost. Learn how to teach the gospel by the Spirit and in the name of Jesus Christ. So doing will truly make you an instrument in the hands of God as a master teacher.

Preparing for marriage

It is a great blessing that you get to serve a mission just before the next chapter of your life, which will include marriage. Many institutions and the Church offer marriage preparation classes. But the best marriage preparation is your mission. When you visit homes, do some thinking about the families you meet. How do they function? What is the father doing or not doing that affects the happiness and growth of the family? What does the wife do to make the family effective? Why is the marriage failing, or why is the marriage just the kind that you would like to have? The things you can learn if you keep your eyes open and seek messages about your future family from the families you are now serving are endless!

You and your companion have been thrust together on your mission. Maybe you thank the Lord every night for the privilege of working with him. Or maybe you pray for the strength to make it to the next transfer. Whatever the case, learn to be unselfish. Be determined to give much more than you receive. Help your companion to succeed and grow from where he is to the higher level. The way you relate to him will be a great opportunity to prepare for the relationship you will have with your future eternal companion.

Dreams bring direction

Even though you must keep focused on the work and joy of your mission, there is still time to dream of the future. What you dream of as you pedal your bike, ride the bus, or wash the dishes will help you keep yourself on course. If you have a girlfriend at home, your dreams of her can be a great positive motivation to you. Your thoughts of her will prompt you to do the things that will cause her to rejoice as she reads your letters. When you think of home, let your mind be filled with how much the folks there are counting on you to be the best missionary serving. Never do anything to let down those whom you love.

The most powerful drive for you to get up on time, to study in the morning, and to get out among the people is the vision you have of those at home who are praying for you and who see you as their hero. Consider their feelings often. Even be homesick to see them. Missionaries who are healthily homesick for two years are usually the missionaries who stay on course from the beginning to the end.

Always have a dream. A dream of the immediate future wherein you long to be another Paul, another Samuel Smith, another Wilford Woodruff, or another elder whom you desire to be like. Then look way out into the future and see yourself as a husband, a father, and a servant of the Lord. Yes, it is good to dream of tomorrow so that you will stay on course today.

Dream of parents

I was raised on a chicken farm. The eggs the hens produced were at the heart of our family's meager income. The more eggs produced, the more income made. It was hard work to care for the chickens—to feed them, to clean the coops, and to gather, box, and take the eggs to market.

The bishop came to my parents to see if it would be possible for me to go on a mission. My father sadly said, "I'm not well, Bishop. I can't continue to care for the chickens. We will have no way to carry on if our son goes."

My mother listened with tears in her eyes. She then sat up straight in her chair and announced, "It is true that my husband can no longer do the work on this farm. But I can. I can care for the chickens. I'm strong enough to do the work, and I will. George can go on a mission."

So I departed. Throughout my mission, not a day passed that I did not think of my mother in the cold or heat carrying feed to the chickens and gathering the eggs. Every time I thought of these things, I went about my mission duties with greater eagerness, more faith, and deeper love. I rejoiced when I received a letter from my mother that read, "The chickens have found out that you are on a mission, and they want to do their part to help. They are laying more eggs than ever before in the history of our farm."

I knew that the Lord was caring for me, my family, and the chickens. I knew that I needed to serve honorably. I knew that I needed to serve with gratitude. I was not a perfect missionary, but I wanted to be!

Dream dreams

It is not good to aspire to church office or position. However, it can be a motivating thing to do a bit of righteous dreaming. As you see the great influence your mission president has in the lives and hearts of the missionaries and the members, you could desire to have such influence someday in your own Church life. It is okay as you pedal your bike down a long road to say to yourself, "Someday it would be great to return to this land that I love so much and to these dear people as the mission president." Thinking such a thought could well give you the power to pedal your bike a little harder, to be more diligent in your studies, to be more expressive of your love, to have more integrity, and to work harder. If what you dream of never happens, it will still result in your being a better husband, father, and friend. Such thinking will make you a more effective leader over a few rows in the Lord's field. And it will make you a better, more loyal follower of others who are called to lead over a larger portion of that field. So don't aspire; do some dreaming of being in positions which will enable you to do good and to bless the lives of others through your service.

15. *Work on Your Attitude*

Keep moving forward

Doing one's best isn't an impossible dream. I'm not talking of perfection. We have obstacles that block us short of that. Our best comes in fighting our way through colds, flat tires, and companion differences. We can't expect the wind to always be with us or all hills to slant downward. We must be able to move forward against the current. Thus, our best is not measured in results so much as in effort. Bursts of speed are refreshing, but the work on a mission is long and it demands a steady and methodical effort. The law of averages guarantees the success of the persistent.

Care deeply

You as a missionary have the right at times to feel bad. When someone rejects you at his door, you should feel bad. When someone turns you away after a discussion, you should feel deeply hurt. When someone almost decides to be baptized and then turns away, you should cry within your soul.

Some build defenses against such hurts. They say, "Oh, well, they had their chance." "We did our best." "Don't worry; this is just a hard mission." "It isn't our fault." "I didn't come out here to get all worried." "Noah didn't do so well either."

Sometimes we joke ourselves into an almost I-don't-care attitude. When that happens, we lose the edge that makes us ever desirous for the better way. If it's been a long time since you helped someone to baptism and that doesn't hurt you, you need to examine your goals. There is a balance that makes life bearable and yet progressive. True, when we try hard and see little success, we shouldn't get down on ourselves, but if such results don't make us feel bad, we need to reevaluate that which we call our heart.

One missionary reported, "Among my greatest sorrows are the disappointments I knew as a missionary in England. Once, after losing several contacts in one neighborhood—all soured by a hateful minister—I felt my heart would break.

"My deep sorrow led me and my companion to a grove of trees in a park. We poured out our sorrows to the Lord. We cast our burdens on him. The Lord heard our prayers. He helped us feel renewed. We were given special help and were led by the Spirit to new families."

It's good to laugh off your woes, but sometimes we laugh too much and cry too little. The Lord might smile when we laugh, but when He knows we hurt and we only have Him to turn to, He cares. How He cares!

Days of discouragement

Sometimes you hit the doldrums of your mission. The excitement of being there ends, and yet there is so much longer to serve. You become discouraged. Almost all of us suffer such feelings at times.

Such feelings are part of the most meaningful lessons we learn as we serve the Lord. What to do about it?

Keep moving ahead. Take things a day at a time. Don't assume that tomorrow you will be as discouraged as today. And just know that next week you will feel much better than now. The physical biorhythms of your body go up and down. The feelings you have today will change soon just because of your body. Maybe you have a cold. Often illness can get you down spiritually as well as physically.

Hang in there. Write down your feelings. List some new goals— some new and higher things that you desire to accomplish or some improvements you wish to make in your personal righteousness. Count your blessings. Write letters to someone who needs encouragement. Do a good deed for your companion, and try to do it in secret. Go to a private room, even the bathroom, and pour your heart out to your Father. Fast. Embrace today. Remember what Christ said, "Sufficient unto today is the evil thereof." Don't worry about what is coming. Do what you have to do today, and all will be well in the future.

Avoid jealousy

A story was once told of a missionary who felt he was qualified to become an assistant to the president. He had that as a goal. He knew the present assistant was soon going home. In his mind, he prepared for this new assignment. Others told him that they felt that he was sure to soon move to the office.

The appointment was made, and it was not him. He was hurt. He felt within his soul that the president had erred. He felt the chosen elder was not as qualified as he was. He had known the appointed elder for many months, and he knew that he had some weaknesses.

In his next interview with the president, he was not his usual enthusiastic self. The president asked him how he felt about the new assistant. The elder decided to express his true and somewhat negative feelings. After hearing him out, the president kindly yet firmly replied, "I wondered why I felt it should be him and not you. I could think of no reason because you were so obviously the right one. But now I know that it was because of these feelings that you just expressed that you were not chosen."

The two sat together in a feeling of understanding and love that only comes when the Spirit of the Lord is there. The elder was advised that how he schooled his feelings on this matter would be the key to fulfilling his destiny of being a great leader in the Church.

Get involved

At college, I sat in the back so I would not be called on. I liked to be an observer in a class and not a participant. My main enjoyment during the class period was when the class was over. One day, I came to the class and saw an empty seat in the back. But this day I could also see a seat at the front. I headed toward my seat at the back. Then I looked again at the seat in the front. I then made a decision that changed my college career. I headed to the seat in the front. I quickly made my way there and sat down right in front of the teacher. By being up close, I felt more involved. I looked intently at the teacher except for the times I had to look down to make sure the notes I was taking were readable. The teacher often looked at me as I nodded agreement. If I did not understand, I asked questions. When the teacher asked for comments, I made his share. I did not want to take over the class or to dominate the discussion. I just wanted to be involved. I found the class was always more interesting and the time went by faster when I made a least one comment.

Don't sit back. Move up close. Even if you have to sit in the back, mentally come up front. Get involved. Often negative feelings come if you feel others are involved and you are not. Don't let that happen. Dive in, not to disrupt with negative words and acts, but to support and to add a positive flavor to what is good.

Support mission programs

Missions, in order to remain alive and growing, often need to initiate new ideas and new programs. The overall message stays the same, but the procedures of implementation change. When the president or other leaders decide to implement a new program, get on board. Don't debunk the ideas that are being taught. Get behind them. Talk them up to others. Make them work. One missionary with a negative attitude about a new program can sour not only himself but also those around him. One missionary with a positive attitude about a new program can influence many others to implement the program with enthusiasm. The more you support what the mission leaders are striving to do, the more you will feel the spirit of oneness in your mission. Be part of the solution in spreading the gospel and not a hindrance. Sometimes you might like to criticize new ideas and to join or even lead the dissenters. You did not come on a mission to do that. You can repent of such feelings. Try the new ideas. As you go though the motions, you will feel the emotions. No idea or program has all the solutions; however, in each program there is more that is positive than is negative. As you embrace the new ideas of others you will be more qualified to someday be the originator of new ways to spread the gospel more effectively.

Avoid comparisons

Two great problems occur when you compare yourself to others. One is that if you are able to do really well, you may fall into feelings of pride. Such ideas will be subtle, and you won't dwell on them. However, you will, in your quiet moments, feel that you have a bit more going for you than others around you have going for them.

The other problem with comparisons is that you may decide that when compared with others, you don't really measure up. In your mind, others are smarter. They come from greater backgrounds. They can speak and teach more powerfully. You may, when making such comparisons, decide, "What's the use? I'm a loser no matter how you slice it up."

My wife once observed:

Three of my children were swinging side by side. The two on the outside were swinging really high then down and high again. They had learned to pump themselves. The littlest of the three was in the center. Unable to pump herself, she was just barely moving because there was a slight wind. Kathryn looked across and said, "I'm keeping up with Devin." Devin looked over at her and said, "I'm keeping up with Kathryn." Little Marinda, who was in the center, looked at each of the other two swinging so much higher than her and said, "I'm just keeping up with myself."

That is the only race that matters—the race which compares what you are now against what you used to be. If you are winning the race of "keeping up with yourself" and even little by little getting ahead of yourself, then you are truly a winner.

Love the mission cars

A story is told of the early days Southern States Mission. Back then, there was a family who was friendly to the missionaries. This family had a white horse named Traveler, which the missionaries could ride to go to distant places to teach and preach. The persecutors of the Church knew the horse was a primary means of transportation for the missionaries. Their hatred of the Church caused them to take it out on the horse. On dark nights, while the missionaries were in a building or a home, these evil doers would sneak up and cut bits off the horse's ears and tail. They scratched it and cut it.

The persecuted horse loved all the missionaries; however, there was one missionary who formed a deep bond with the noble animal. Finally this missionary's time to serve ended, and after a sad farewell to the horse, he returned home. After some four years the missionary was traveling on business to the area of his former mission. At the conclusion of his business, he traveled fifty extra miles to visit the family. As he neared the farmhouse, he was excited to see his friends. He hoped the horse would still be there.

After a joyous reunion with the family, the missionary inquired about the horse. He was told that the old steed was now lame, but was still alive. He told the family that he would like to go alone out to the field where the horse was standing. The missionary felt deep emotions of love as he walked slowly toward his old friend. He advanced to within fifty yards of where the horse was grazing with his head down. The missionary lovingly called out the name, "Traveler." The horse quickly raised his head and peered toward the missionary. The old animal recognized his friend. The missionary ran toward the horse, and the gallant horse hobbled forward. A moment later, the missionary embraced the animal's neck, and the horse nudged the missionary with his nose. The horse and the missionary were together again, and they were happy. The family who followed close behind had never witnessed such a joyous reunion

Your car is like your horse. Talk to your car. Give it a name. It is a missionary. Treat it with great love. Keep it clean. Drive it with care. Someday in several years you might see it in a junkyard. Go over to it. It will know you. Well maybe not. But your car is sacred. Treat it that way and it will take you to sacred places and treasured experience.

16. *Love Missionary Couples*

The joy of couples

"Kids, your mom and I are going on a mission."

There are embraces, tears, and the words "That's so wonderful! You'll do great! The people will love you."

"Where will you go, Grandpa? How long will you be gone?"

"Mamma, I don't want Grandma and Grandpa to go."

"Now, children. Heavenly Father needs them."

"But who will take me fishing and to the park?"

You have second thoughts, but only momentarily. "Grandma and I will write to you. We'll send you pictures."

After the journey of many miles, you are almost there. What will the mission president be like? Will he ask more of you than you can give? You meet him. He is so kind and understanding. You love both him and his wife already. You feel so much better now.

But where will he send you? Will the people there accept you? Where will you live? Will you even be able to find your way there? You don't know a living soul there. "I wonder if the house back home is okay. I hope the furnace works." A quick thought of your front room at home. The kitchen, the garden, the grandchildren. A surge of real homesickness fills your heart.

Finally there it is. There's your new city. The handsome young zone leaders meet you. These young men are so mature, so confident, and so friendly.

"This is your apartment. If it's unsuitable, you can look around and get another."

So small, so humble, yet it seems so much like the right place.

Unpack. The president of the small branch stops by. He seems so glad you are here.

The first week at church. Not a large group, but so humble, so full of appreciation. Many invitations to visit members. Such instant love.

"Please come by me. My husband will want to meet you. I'll bet you are the ones who will get him into the Church."

Time goes by, but only slowly at first. Weeks, then months. The branch president asks for your advice on a number of matters. He wants to succeed but is so new in Church leadership. All the training you had in the Church at home means so much here where leadership is sparse. The president seems so appreciative of the support you give. The number of people at church increases. The spirit seems so much better now.

A baptism. Such a good husband and father. You've never seen a happier family.

Now you are teaching the man who works at the grocery store and also the postman. The landlord is also asking questions. Your lives are entwining with other lives. Thoughts of home are less frequent.

A letter from home contains pictures of the children. They seem to have grown. You read: "Johnny said, 'My Grandma and Grandpa are on a mission. When I get big I'm going on a mission too.'" You feel a joy which is unsurpassed.

Problems! These people need so much help. A long talk with a married couple headed for divorce. They seemed to feel better after the talk. "Heavenly Father, we love them so much. Please help them."

And then a crushing blow. It is a call from the mission president. A transfer. How can you leave here? Tears at a farewell party. You are ready to leave your apartment and your town. Many come to bid you good-bye. As you look into their tear-filled eyes, you say, "We'll be back—after our mission, we'll be back."

"God bless you," they call out to you. "We'll never forget you."

A new area. More confidence this time. The cycle starts again.

A call from home at Christmas. "Grandpa, I can't wait until spring, 'cause Mom says you'll be home."

Spring is coming soon. Please slow down the time. You still have much to do. These people need a chapel. The president is trying so hard. The two factions of the branch seem to be coming together at last. You love it here. The family you taught and baptized is struggling, but they are determined to make it to the temple in a year. This place is so beautiful. This little apartment is home. The flowers in the window are doing well.

The young elders are like your own sons. You love to feed them. They rely on you a great deal. They are wonderful.

The president says he doesn't know what he'd do without you. He's such a good man.

The other ten couples and you meet together for a conference. You decide you'd meet each year after your missions. You never have known such wonderful couples. They came here from all over the United States. They were farmers, coal miners, lawyers, businessmen, hunting guides, handymen, and teachers. They all have grandchildren and gardens. You could talk with them forever. You love to get together with them, but at the end of such meetings, you can hardly bear to say so long.

Sad news. One of the elders whom you saw at the conference is in the hospital. He had a heart attack. But he told his wife he'd recover because he had received a blessing from the president. He's doing better. You are fasting and praying for him. He is a choice man and his wife is like an angel.

Time is closing in on you. A farewell party is planned. The grandchildren write often. They are so excited.

You'll be home in time to plant the garden—but somehow that doesn't seem as important as it once did. The people will move out of your house the week before you get home. What will you ever do with that big house? This little apartment seems just the right size.

The farewell party. A special song composed by a newly activated sister. The words are about you. They are words of love and appreciation. You both cry. You've never felt so needed, so loved.

Farewell talks. Power with words has never been like this. As you speak you express your feelings as best you can but then you pause, for no words will come. Then a testimony that has never been as strong.

The parting. It would be unbearable except for the hope in the words "We'll come back. Don't worry, we'll come back." You journey away from the people you love. Going home is not what you thought it would be.

The homecoming. No one could really know how much the mission meant to you. From now on almost every conversation you will ever have will include a thought of the mission. Hoeing corn and washing dishes leave time for thinking. What did you ever think of or talk about before your mission?

"What if we'd never gone, Honey? What if we'd never met those folks?" The thought is too hard to bear.

Yes, you come two by two; you labor two by two; you perform miracles two by two. You fall more and more in love. You depend on each other. You know joy and sorrow two by two. You are loved by the people as one. And then when your mission is done, you head home to your first home. You now have a second home and almost a new family. Your life now will never be the same.

Yes, these are the couples. The special people who come and who care, who love and are loved, and who will be called blessed forever. To them the word mission will always bring back many memories. May God bless the couples forever.

About the Author

George D. Durrant was born and raised in American Fork, Utah. He has served in many capacities in the LDS Church Educational System. For several years he was director of Priesthood Genealogy for the Church.

In addition, he served for three years as president of the Missionary Training Center in Provo, Utah, and has taught religion classes at Brigham Young University.

Brother Durrant is the author of more than a dozen books, including *Don't Forget the Star* and the best-selling *Scones for the Heart, Love at Home—Staring Father.*

He is married to the former Marilyn Burnham. They are the parents of eight children.